CHALLENGE AND
CHANGE IN THE
MILITARY:
GENDER AND
DIVERSITY ISSUES

Edited by
Franklin C. Pinch, Allister T. MacIntyre,
Phyllis Browne, and Alan C. Okros

CANADIAN DEFENCE ACADEMY PRESS

Canadian Forces Leadership Institute

 Canadian Defence Academy Press
PO Box 17000 Stn Forces
Kingston, Ontario   K7K 7B4

Published for Canadian Forces Leadership Institute by the Wing Publishing Office,
17 Wing Winnipeg.

Second printing February 2006.

Library and Archives Canada Cataloguing in Publication

Main entry under title :

Challenge and change in the military : gender and diversity issue

Third and final book to be published in the "Challenge and change
in the military" series that resulted from an international conference
held in Kingston, Ont. in Oct. 2002.—Cf. Acknowledgements
ISBN 0-662-39996-X
Cat. no. D2-166/2005E

1. Women soldiers – Congresses.
2. Armed forces – Minorities – Congresses.
3. Discrimination in employment – Congresses.
4. Sociology, Military – Congresses.
5. Canada – Armed Forces – Women – Congresses.
6. Canada – Armed Forces – Minorities – Congresses.
I. Pinch, Franklin C. (Frank Conrad), 1940-   .
II. Canadian Forces Leadership Institute.

UB418.C44 2005   355.0082   C2005-980106-9

Printed in Canada.

3 5 7 9 10 8 6 4 2

TABLE OF CONTENTS

ACKNOWLEDGEMENTS

In October 2002, the Inter-University on Armed Forces and Society (IUS): Canada Region, in cooperation with the Canadian Forces Leadership Institute (CFLI) and the Queen's University Defence Management Studies Program (DMSP), hosted its first international conference in Kingston, Ontario. This is the third and last book to be published in the *Challenge and Change in the Military* series that resulted from the Conference.

IUS Canada is a regional organization within the IUS that was founded by the noted military sociologist, Morris Janowitz, at the University of Chicago in the 1960s. It is dedicated to independent social science research and scholarship that focuses both on the relationship between the military and society and on the military institution itself. The Fellows of the IUS, numbering more than 800, represent a broad range of disciplines and some 50 countries, and are involved in the study of armed forces and society within academic institutions, research establishments and military forces around the world. The President at the time of the conference was Dr. David R. Segal, Distinguished Professor of Sociology at the University of Maryland, later succeeded by Dr. John Allen Williams of Loyola University. IUS Canada was established in 1981, and the Canadian Chair was Dr. Franklin C. Pinch; his successor is Dr. Alan Okros, former Director of CFLI and Associate Professor in the Department of Military Psychology and Leadership, Royal Military College of Canada (RMC). Lieutenant-Colonel David Last, current Registrar of RMC was Program Director of the 2002 IUS Canada Conference, and Lois Jordan, Manager of the IUS Canada Secretariat, was Conference Coordinator.

CFLI was established in 2001, with a broad mandate for leadership concept development, leadership research and cooperation with academic institutions and international research associations; its current director is Colonel Bernd Horn, an IUS fellow. The Queen's University Defence Management Studies Program (DMSP), chaired since its inception in 1996 by Dr. Douglas Bland, is one of 16 university chairs sponsored by the department of National Defence's Security and Defence Forum (SDF).

We wish to acknowledge the collaborative efforts of Douglas Bland, who was lead editor of the first volume; and David Last, who was lead editor of the second volume; as well as those of this book's contributing authors, in planning the *Challenge and Change* series. We are grateful for the institutional support of the Canadian Defence Academy and its agency, CFLI, for making publication of this document possible. Our specific thanks to Trisha Mitchell and Joanne Simms for their administrative and clerical support in the early stages of this project. Finally, our gratitude goes to Moira Jackson, Queen's University, for her able editing and perceptive comments on the various chapters of this manuscript, and to Brian Selmeski for his copy editing efforts. The patience, professionalism, and hard work of all are appreciated.

The Editors
March 2005

FOREWORD

As with previous publications issued by the Canadian Defence Academy (CDA) and the Canadian Forces Leadership Institute (CFLI), this book represents our ongoing commitment to the education of Canadian Forces (CF) members. It is a direct response to our recognition that there must be a mechanism in place to allow the dissemination of high quality scholarly and professional works. These CDA / CFLI publications contribute to a distinct Canadian body of operational leadership and profession of arms knowledge. They serve to enhance professional development within the Department of National Defence (DND) and the CF, and offer a method to educate the public with respect to the significant contribution of their military.

In the case of this publication, the chapters were selected from a series of presentations offered at the Canadian Inter-University Seminar (IUS) on Armed Forces and Society hosted by the CFLI in Kingston, Ontario. Two related themes thread their way throughout these chapters: gender and diversity. These topics continue to be of critical importance for the military and will always be of importance for any organization that has a desire to maximize its effectiveness. Diversity, in all its forms and guises, is a contemporary concern and a subject of heated debate; it influences change and transformation, and presents challenges for governments, employers, and institutions of liberal-democratic societies. Similarly, the subject of gender integration has a lengthy and often ignoble history that has generated considerable discourse.

We believe that the Canadian Forces have led the way with our innovative approaches to all aspects of diversity and employment equity. We have opened countless doors that remain closed in other western militaries and we have systematically removed employment barriers for the citizens of Canada. The scholarly articles captured in this book provide intellectual insights into diversity and gender integration. The authors demonstrate a passion for these subjects that will be of interest to academia and the general population alike.

P.R. Hussey
Major-General, Commander CDA

PREFACE

At first glance, readers might question why the Canadian Forces Leadership Institute (CFLI) would release a book on gender integration and diversity. After all, these two topics do not give the appearance of having a direct relationship to leadership or leader behaviours. In their purest form, gender and diversity can simply be viewed as states of being; one is either male or female and groups are either diverse or not. However, leadership is not just about influencing followers to accomplish a mission. Effective leaders recognize that people are different. They also understand that one approach does not fit all, and that both diversity and gender integration within groups are strengths not weaknesses.

Quite simply, diversity is all about people and their differences, whether these differences are real or imagined. Leaders need to recognize that there is a natural human tendency to categorize people in a way that helps us to make sense out of our world. We assign the people we meet to the category, or categories, they most resemble. These groupings may be extremely broad (e.g., Canadian versus American), or based on aspects like race, religion, or gender. We further complicate things in the military by adding many additional categories (e.g., Army/Navy/Air Force; operational/support). The categories we use come with a set of assumptions and attitudes about the people within a given group. These attitudes influence how we think about the people in a group, how we feel about them, and how we are likely to behave in their presence. Leaders who understand this principle will be able to anticipate how followers will react in the presence of other groups and be able to use this as an advantage when necessary (e.g., when group membership becomes critically salient at sports events).

As indicated earlier, diversity is about differences, real or perceived, among groups. In any social context, one group may become dominant. Throughout recorded history, people have used their views and beliefs about other groups as a form of justification for discrimination, for the denial of access to certain resources or to treat their views as being irrelevant to the on-going affairs of nations, communities, institutions, or organizations. True leaders need to appreciate this fundamental aspect of human nature.

B. Horn, Colonel
Director
Canadian Forces Leadership Institute

AN INTRODUCTION TO CHALLENGE AND CHANGE IN THE MILITARY:
GENDER AND DIVERSITY ISSUES

FRANKLIN C. PINCH

INTRODUCTION

Diversity in the military is a complex subject, both conceptually and in terms of its more practical, managerial implications. It represents one of the most significant and difficult challenges for human resource management that military leaders have faced over the past two or three decades. Greater diversity in recruitment, development, and employment has challenged traditional military institutional norms, values, beliefs, and attitudes. Human resource philosophies, policies, programs, and practices have been adapted and revised. This volume adds to the accumulating evidence of the progress that has been made in understanding and managing diversity in the armed forces and the problems that remain unresolved. Its main focus is the full integration of women, which some analysts see as the most problematic; many nations have yet to resolve key gender-related issues.[1]

This introduction has two main purposes. The first is to introduce the reader to the topics of gender and diversity and to convey their importance at this stage of the evolution of Western militaries. The second is to provide an overview of the individual chapters, along with brief editorial comments.

Diversity (or heterogeneity), in all its forms and guises, is a topic of contemporary concern and debate, as well as an influence for change and transformation; as such, it presents challenges for governments, employers, and institutions of liberal-democratic societies. Diversity is about differences, *real or perceived*, among groups. The consequences of belonging to a particular group are likely to be political, social or economic. In any social context (a nation, a community, an institution, or an organization, for example), one group may become dominant. A well-known dichotomy holds that dominant cultural and social groups (in-groups), regardless of how they may have gained such status or legitimacy, tend to view their own norms, values, outlooks, and ways of doing things as normal, right, or even superior, and those of others (out-groups) as deficient or inferior, at least in some respects. Throughout recorded history, various in-groups have used these views, and other justifications, to discriminate against others in a variety of ways, to deny them access to certain resources, or to treat them as irrelevant to the on-going affairs of nations, communities, institutions, or employment organizations.[2]

Differences of continuing importance include those of age, gender, sexual orientation, family status, disability status, language, race, national or ethnic origin, and religion. Some are biologically determined (skin colour, sex, etc.). But virtually all of the differences that are important to the workplace (work ethic and habits, leadership and managerial capability, preferences for certain type of work, intellectual orientation, etc.) are developed through education, training, and other forms of socialization and experience. Moreover, there is such wide variation within apparently homogeneous groups that a general impression or stereotype of a group tells us very little about any given individual. The same holds for generalizations from an individual to a group. These considerations apply to gender differences, which are given the lion's share of attention in this volume, and to other types of diversity that are dealt with both tacitly and explicitly in two of the chapters.

THE CURRENT SITUATION

Social, political, technological, and economic developments over the past several decades have undermined the power of dominant groups in the West. There is recognition of the need to allow full access to the social and institutional mainstream of various Western societies. Women have made perhaps the most dramatic gains in participation rates in all employment and societal organizations, including the military.[3] Civil rights campaigns and other social movements have stimulated legislative changes that have advanced the rights of women and others in the workplace. Governments and the courts have been working towards social justice and equality of opportunity. Barriers to participation in employment organizations are being removed.[4] Moreover, in an increasingly global context, both public- and private-sector organizations have begun to recognize the advantages of a more diverse workforce.[5]

Debate continues at all levels as to how far diversity can or should go, and how it will be managed – nowhere more hotly than around the question of the military. One of the latest comparative analyses of this topic indicates that views differ considerably across national governments and among military leaders and scholars of armed forces and society.[6] The military's deliberately powerful socialization system and processes create and reinforce a "tight culture" in which in-groups undoubtedly develop. One of the intended consequences of these socializing influences is the development of the cohesive, highly motivated groups deemed necessary for group survival and successful missions. One unintended – often negative – result is the emergence of norms, values, and stereotypes that exclude the "not like us" groups. To some extent, the internal policy debates, including those in this volume, revolve around how militaries might maintain an intentional socialization regime – so as to optimize "requisite" group characteristics – in a way that brings other social and cultural groups into the mainstream by incorporating essential aspects of them.

CONTENT OVERVIEW - GENERAL

This volume deals with the concepts and theory of "diversity management" relevant to policy change, as the military responds to macro-social and legal pressures to include women. It examines the barriers that continue to prevent full integration, including those associated with masculine cultural norms. A sample from France offers the perceptions and experiences of military women vis-à-vis expectations of them by men and the military. Related to perceptions and expectations, as well as to diversity-management concerns, is a cross-national examination of issues such as harassment, sex and gender, and abuse of authority. This has become a greater concern as more women participate in the military and expand into non-traditional roles and occupational specialties.

One chapter examines demographic changes and discusses their policy implications for the Canadian military. Changing socio-demographic patterns help to determine the degree to which diversity is of concern in a given nation. They also help to determine what future strategic human resource objectives and priorities should be. Diverse groups may have conflicting values, which must be managed carefully if cultural minorities are to be recruited and retained. It is from that perspective that the final chapter examines the "value fit" between Aboriginal groups and the military.

OVERVIEW - INDIVIDUAL CHAPTERS

Chapter One

Gwyn Harries-Jenkins makes the link between the pressures from a changing society, the changes in managerial philosophies and styles, and the concepts used by social scientists, in discussing the significance of change over the past three decades. Even though his focus is on "gender", he provides a conceptual basis for a discussion of diversity in general. By reference to the *Institutional-Occupational* models of change and development in the military institution – introduced in the 1970s by Charles Moskos and modified through continuing research – he traces the changes in policy developments and other issues relevant to the integration of women into Western militaries.

According to the author, the Institutional model, which derives its legitimacy from traditional military norms, depicts a "paternalistic...custodial management style". It came under societal pressure in the 1960s, and the military turned its human resources policies towards the Occupational model and the greater inclusion of previously excluded groups, including women. The business motivation for this change was the need to maintain an operationally effective force that was able to meet new challenges in the face of persistent shortfalls in technical personnel. The equity case reflected socio-legal demands for equality in employment opportunities. As Harries-Jenkins indicates, the increase in the dimensions of diversity is considered to be a measure of overall quality.

In examining the diversity thesis as it applies to gender, Harries-Jenkins sets out the relationship between macro- and micro-level personnel policy changes over time in a number of nations. While there are national variations, he sees a four-stage, sequential policy change: from the total exclusion of women from all or most military occupational specialties through partial exclusion and qualified inclusion to full inclusion. Women have generally been relegated to support roles, the ground combat-arms occupations having been the most resistant to the inclusion of women. Harries-Jenkins points to the importance of Stage 4 employment in the core operational military specialties of the direct fighting arms as a prerequisite for advancement to more senior positions at both the commissioned and non-commissioned officer levels. This has been a limiting factor for women in uniform. In a number of countries, women's participation in combat specialties has been cyclical at best, and progress stalled all together once the wartime crises passed (as occurred, for example, in the former Soviet Union after World War II). Some countries, such as the U.K. and the U.S., have developed personnel policies at the micro level of partial inclusion, a restriction that is consistent with the traditional Institutional model and that conveys the "ideal military image of the physically strong, emotionally tough, masculine war hero". Such policies are internally sustained by the cultural influence of a combat masculine war-fighting (CMW) model, shaped largely by men. Harries-Jenkins contrasts this with the diversity model, which "starts from the fundamental premise that the organization, structure, and management of the military reflect the norms and values of civilian society." This represents the movement to "an inclusionary ideal-type image, which is created and reinforced by the adopted micro-level personnel policies."

The diversity model, however, is "noticeably complex" and depends on a balance between socio-legal demands and what is required to maintain "combat capability". Harries-Jenkins sees three concepts as relevant to developing micro-policy that will optimize diversity: tokenism, equal opportunities, and positive discrimination. According to leading analysts, women must number 15 percent of an organization to be considered more than a token. Most Western militaries do not meet this standard. Women are still being treated, especially in the operational combatant areas, as highly visible "tokens", rather than as fully contributing military members. The author cites research that shows several negative outcomes from this absence of gender neutrality, including acute work stress for the women involved. As a crisis organization, the military must be able to respond capably when called upon. Arguably, an inclusive, gender-integrated approach increases the risk of not having enough personnel available; a number of less-than-perfect policy options may reduce this risk. Various policy dilemmas and competing points of view affect the recruiting and retention policies that attempt to optimize equal opportunity for men and women under the diversity-management concept, while still meeting operational effectiveness standards. Another challenge lies in the generally small percentage of women in the military, in the direct-combat specialties (where permitted), and at senior rank levels.

One possible solution to both problems lies in implementing policies that better consolidate "civilian working practices, establishment of (acceptable) role models, image-building, and cultural change...." Though consistent with a diversity model, such practices run counter to "Institutional" policies of career advancement that emphasize experience and seniority. They may create other difficulties, such as causing resentment and damaging the perception of the military image as unique. Also, positive discrimination policies do not achieve a good balance between the "business case" and the "equity case".

Harries-Jenkins regards the contemporary military as still developing toward a diversity model, one plagued by ambiguity and uncertainty. The poor fit between the current culture and the policy goals of diversity suggests a need for concentrated effort on cultural change at the strategic level. He points out, however, that there is little agreement on how cultural change can be effected and that any alternatives proposed have their own drawbacks. In the final analysis, external macro-policies founded on socio-legal bases must be coordinated with micro-policies – that is, military responses to external demands. The key is to enact policy that will create the image and the role models necessary for gender diversity to stabilize and progress. Both the Institutional and Occupational models retain the emphasis on the traditional "functional imperative" and a male-centred bias toward societal norms and military service. Harries Jenkins questions the appropriateness of such models and images in concluding:

> Today...not only is the pertinence of conservative, male-dominated anachronistic models questioned, but their very conceptual validity is in doubt. The diversity model argues that, in a situation of free choice within all-volunteer forces, heterogenic influences and demanded represen-tativeness, the primary functional military objectives of

combat effectiveness have to be matched by acceptance of difference. Inclusiveness and heterogeneity, rather than exclusiveness and homogeneity, have to prevail.[7]

Chapter Two

Karen Davis and Brian McKee relate the debate over the full implementation of the gender-diversity model explicitly to arguments opposing women in combat roles. Their stated position is "that the real hurdle for women in participating fully in the military today has little to do with their physical and mental abilities but rather revolves around social and cultural issues characterizing the 'warrior framework'." They also argue for a strategic approach to basing decisions as to women's roles on credible research-based information, rather than on "myths", biases, and outdated arguments.

The chapter is rooted in what has transpired in Canada since the 1960s and, like Harries-Jenkins, Davis and McKee link progress in women's integration to societal change and public support, human rights legislation, the Charter of Rights and Freedoms, and tribunal rulings that have extended women's participation to all roles and environments. Various restrictions persist even where formal inclusion policies are in effect (e.g., in the form of unsubstantiated physical and other requirements that prevent women from entering elite combat or special forces units). Whether formal or informal, these restrictions are associated with the "over-emphasis on the warrior ethos focused predominantly on combat operations and war-fighting", without proper regard for the broader range of contemporary roles in peace support, humanitarian efforts, and domestic operations.

The traditional reasons for excluding women from combat roles, according to Davis and McKee, revolve around questions such as those posed at the end of the 1980s by the Heritage Foundation in the U.S. These focus on the physical and mental suitability of women, their impact on cohesion and effectiveness, readiness to deploy on short notice, public and personal attitudes toward women in combat, and their interest in entering combat roles. They address each of these briefly.

The authors cite research that casts doubt on the assumption that women cannot meet the physical and mental rigors of combat; women have shown themselves to be superior to men in such areas as physical endurance, and have demonstrated, with appropriate training and development, vast increases in physical abilities. The authors also provide evidence that, despite differing standards for men and women, physical fitness tests in Canada provide fair predictions of the ability of each to perform to a military occupational standard. Further, they maintain that the distinct differences in physical strength and stamina between men and women are largely irrelevant to meeting the demands of military performance.

With regard to the long-standing traditional notion that women's participation in combat roles would have a negative impact on cohesion and operational effectiveness, Davis and McKee indicate that many of the anticipated problems (e.g., fraternization and sexual misconduct) either have been overstated or can be handled by appropriate education and human resource policies. Recent studies in the U.S. and U.K. show that the presence of various proportions of women affects cohesion in distinctly minor ways, if at all. Maintenance of cohesion and operational effectiveness are determined more by other factors, such as leadership and teamwork, and there are examples of women serving successfully in combat roles without degrading cohesion and operational effectiveness. Nor do Davis and McKee accept the arguments that having women in combat roles is necessarily more acceptable in militaries that do not frequently go to war (e.g., Canada, Scandinavia) than in those that do (e.g., the U.K. and U.S.). Also, by and large, despite fears to the contrary, servicewomen taken captive have not been treated worse than their male counterparts. Overall, these fear-related exclusions of women from combat roles are seen to be based largely on cultural and religious factors unique to the nations involved.

With respect to readiness to deploy on short notice, there are many reasons besides pregnancy and motherhood for this to be a problem for women. For example, while the non-deployable rate in the US Army is quite high, the overall pregnancy rate is comparatively very low. After deployment, pregnancy has made it necessary to remove women, but so have a number of other administrative and medical conditions affecting both genders. As to replacement, it is easier to replace a combat soldier than it is another technical specialist. While women are twice as likely as men to cite family and child-rearing as reasons for not joining the military, those who do choose to join are basing their choice on motives that are similar to the reasons for joining cited by men. Further, the burden of children and family is increasingly becoming a joint parental responsibility. These issues are important to motivation and morale for all service members who have such obligations, and human resource policies aimed at mitigating such problems as maternity, absence, and replacement are an integral part of the contemporary military.

As to whether or not the arduous physical demands will deter women from entering combat roles, Davis and McKee argue that the research does not convincingly associate low interest among women with lack of confidence in their physical capabilities (men's interest in the combat arms has often been low as well). Rather, it may be attributed to the degree of familiarity with what combat roles entail, since interest-level differences between men and women without experience are less pronounced. Thus, giving women more exposure to combat roles – especially if there are successful role models for women – may raise their interest and narrow that gap between men and women.

In the second part of the chapter, Davis and McKee turn to a critical examination of the "warrior framework". They argue that developments in military policy and doctrine are increasingly dominated by the terms "warrior ethos", "warrior culture", and "warrior spirit". The warrior framework (which Harries-Jenkins' chapter referred to as the CMW model) is combat-focused and has not been objectively tested against the need for both operational effectiveness and gender equality in the post-modern military. Citing US and Canadian authors, Davis and McKee argue that the warrior framework has gained emphasis and legitimacy as a schema for describing the entire military. This, they argue, runs counter to trends in the spectrum of mission requirements that now fall to operational combat personnel. As well, changes in weapons and other technology obviate the need for the "brute strength and brawn" emphasized by the warrior culture. In this regard, the prototype for the ideal UN soldier that has emerged from Swedish research departs considerably from the CMW model. Such changes make it imperative that military role- and job-labelling be based on *bona fide* occupational requirements, backed by systematic research.

In their conclusion, Davis and McKee raise questions about the role of the military in the broader security environment, the influence of technology, the privatization of military support and operational roles, and their likely effects on military ethos, the warrior framework, and the role of women. They recognize that progress has been made in women's integration but judge it as slow compared with that of the civilian world. Nevertheless, they see "warrior creep" as being unwarranted by current and future military requirements, inimical to progress in women's integration, and obstructive to the participation of some men as well.

Chapter Three

Katia Sorin gives us a more personalized view of what gender diversity means from the perspective of women as they attempt to cope with the demands of the masculine military environment in France. Sorin's background, though based on specific time periods, reflects the stage process described by Harries-Jenkins, in which women were at first excluded but through legislation and policy have now achieved full formal inclusion in the various services and corps. However, reflecting the views of Chapters One and Two, she notes that formal inclusion policies and full acceptance of gender diversity have not solved all the problems of women's participation in the military.

Although it may be assumed from the organizational perspective that gender integration has been achieved, Sorin documents sufficiently high levels of tension and conflict to indicate that women still perceive their acceptance – both formal and informal – to be grudging rather than whole-hearted. She points out that the French military (like most others) has been seen traditionally as a male preserve, in which "military service was regarded as the most important phase in a young man's progression to manhood." As in other nations, the masculine image and qualities of the military stand in stark contrast to the feminine qualities attributed to women in French society. Sorin asserts that recent reforms in France's defence establishment, including the expansion of women's roles, threaten both the image and the raison d'être of military service for male soldiers. An underlying assumption of the study on which the chapter is based is that women entering non-traditional military roles are "stigmatized" and, indeed, this is reflected in their responses to military life.

At time of writing, women made up approximately 10 percent of the French military and were restricted only from submarine service and, for non-commissioned officers (NCOs), from the Gendarmerie Mobile. For a variety of reasons, including their educational qualifications, they are still mainly concentrated in the traditional roles of administrative, clerical, and medical services. There are considerable variations based on rank and type of entry, with women virtually absent from the more senior ranks. In general, women differ from men in age, seniority, marital status, family status, and whether they have career or contract status (women are more likely to be on contract status and, on average, are more junior than men). Considerable intragroup differences exist among the women themselves, both in background and in career status. Increasing numbers are employed in non-traditional military occupations but there are still few women in operational combat areas. While the study sample of women reflects these distributions to some extent, the emphasis is on the 70 percent of all ranks employed in operational environments. The sample includes both conscripts and those who have volunteered and are on variable-length contracts.

Among Sorin's many findings is the fact that women have not been granted "willing" access to military academies, which provide the foundation for positions of responsibility. The "contract market" for officer entry channels women into support areas and away from the "heavy symbolic operational" content. Further, "the pathway to high command is still held to a very large extent by male hands."

Expansion of women's roles is not considered part of an egalitarian trend in the French forces. "Differential work assignments" for men and women and the "internal gender-determined structuring of occupations" provide evidence of discriminatory practices. Double standards that place women at a disadvantage vis-à-vis their male counterparts are also seen to exist elsewhere. For example, in the major military academy at Saint-Cyr, where women are in the distinct minority, male-female relations are described as largely confrontational. A highly unequal war between the sexes is fostered by the attitudes and actions of male superiors and instructors, who are perceived to not support women or to not take appropriate disciplinary action against males. Women feel they are treated like outsiders, as invisible; they are otherwise scorned, demeaned, insulted, and subjected to sexual jokes and innuendo.

On the other hand, some environments are welcoming to women. Some even treat them preferentially. In other instances, males who have served with them judge them to have performed effectively in operational environments. Overall, however, the picture painted by Sorin's research is one of women struggling to achieve their legitimate place in an organization that does not fully accept them, that reminds them of their "different" status, and that forces them to be "continually on their guard, on the defensive; they can take nothing for granted—everything must be fought for." For women, such conditions represent inter- and intrapersonal conflicts and raise reservations, doubts, feelings of guilt and inadequacy, and the sense that they are not being treated as individuals but, rather, are being defined and assimilated as a group by men.

Virtually all women want to be "regarded as soldiers in every respect" and to "establish good healthy, professional relationships with their male colleagues." These aims are sometimes achieved. Since women, like men, represent a heterogeneous population, gender integration does not have the same meaning for all of them. They respond differentially to service conditions, social arrangements/events, and the on-going integration process in general. For example, women have differing reactions to offensive caricatures or pornographic material that are part of the male military environment; they also differ in the degree to which they want to express their femininity as part of their military identities. Some want to emphasize it and show they are different from men; others want to emphasize their professional military identity, as men do; still others aim for an equal balance between their personal (feminine) and professional (military) identities. Each represents a way of coping with the military environment, and these tend to vary according to such factors as age, rank, experience, and family status.

Sorin concludes that gender issues in the French armed forces revolve around integration and conflict. The integration aspects refer to women's apparent progress in gaining acceptance as full, professional members of the French armed forces. However, this military organizational perspective is more often "hypothetical" than real. Since it is a male-defined environment, the military is often hostile to women. Women do not adapt to the armed forces as easily as men. Although this will vary on an individual basis, specific factors include: rejection, isolation, and unhealthy attitudes held mainly by men, but also by some women. These factors are especially pronounced within the operational combatant sectors of the forces. Conflict between the social and personal identity and the professional identity is not experienced as acutely by men, and women experience conflict in their relationships both with men and with other women.

Sorin contends that a better understanding of the elements involved in women's integration – one that also considers male views– requires comprehensive research. Effective human resource policies are necessary to make women's transition and integration less problematic. But since women do not represent a homogeneous group, there is no "magic formula" to eliminate inherent interpersonal and identity conflicts. Sorin believes that the adversity faced by women participating in the French armed forces and the institutional changes that must be effected to support their true integration are "universal" and can be generalized to other militaries.

Chapter Four

As earlier noted, exclusion from the military, or any other organization, is a form of discrimination against groups or individuals, based primarily on their ascriptive characteristics or affiliations. One form of discrimination, which is also one of the more serious, is harassment in all its various types and manifestations. Nicola Holden and

Karen Davis offer a cross-national look at the degree to which harassment is a problem. This provides a view of the dynamics that can make life in uniform unpleasant, demeaning, and demotivating.

The chapter is based on comparative analyses involving Australia, Canada, New Zealand, and the U.S., four of the more progressive nations with respect to so-called "gender integration". These countries also share characteristics that have been influenced by "a predominantly white, male, heterosexual culture and Judeo-Christian tradition", and each has populations and militaries that reflect a range of diversity. Their militaries are all legislatively mandated to include women, and all have counter-harassment policies. Survey results in these countries provide a baseline of the incidence and types of harassment and measures of effectiveness of existing counter-harassment policies, programs, and practices as they have been applied in the various militaries or separate services concerned.

The authors begin by outlining the methodological problems they encountered in attempting a direct comparative analysis across nations, some of which are related to variable time periods (1987 to 2000) among the various surveys: differing definitions of harassment, forms and content of the underlying surveys, the coverage populations and samples, and the manner in which results were reported. All of these affect the precision of the comparison. A major strength is that this set of time-series analyses within countries provides internal as well as external comparisons. Owing to difficulties in making direct comparisons, however, the authors treat each country's analysis as a case study. Even so, the overall results lead to some convincing conclusions about the direction of this major indicator of progress (or lack thereof) in management of gender diversity.

Notwithstanding the variability in methodology and the manner in which the results were reported across nations, there was general agreement on what constitutes harassment. The results indicate that all forms of harassment have constituted a significant problem for each of the militaries. Sexual harassment continues to be reported, most commonly as "repeatedly told sexual stories or offensive jokes" (Australia), "sexual teasing, jokes and remarks" (Canada, U.S.) and "sexual teasing, jokes, remarks or questions" (New Zealand). Actual or attempted rape, sexual assault, and violence were the least likely to be reported, but all nations reported some of these incidents. Incident rates varied cross-nationally according to type of harassment measured, and by gender and military rank, among other demographic characteristics. Proportionately more women than men were subjected to the various forms of harassment measured. However, where longitudinal data were available, the trend shows an overall decrease in the reported incident rates of harassment (except racial, which remained the same in the US forces) for both women and men throughout the 1990s.

The authors offer several possible explanations for this decrease, among them the positive effects of prevention programs, the creation and implementation of counter-harassment policies, and visible involvement by military leaders. Less positive reasons include fear of consequences by victims who report it (e.g., concern about remaining anonymous) and lack of confidence that leaders will fairly and effectively address the problem. Despite the above reservations, Holden and Davis conclude that repeated surveys are more likely to produce a realistic picture of harassment than the formal complaint system, since the latter places the burden for eradicating harassment on the more vulnerable members of the organization rather than on the leaders and managers, where it belongs.

Chapter Five

Underlying the entire notion of diversity are demographic trends and characteristics, both nationally and internationally. Christian

Leuprecht reminds us of the relationship between the demographic make-up of society and diversity management. He draws a connection between continuing instability in human resource management resulting from a narrow recruitment base, and the need to attract military participants from a broader, more diverse pool of potential recruits in Canada. This is consistent with Harries-Jenkins' more general finding of persistent military human resource shortfalls and ascendant diversity concepts and policies. Although Leuprecht deals explicitly with the Canadian case, he notes similar demographic influences in other Western societies. For example, the post-Second World War "baby boom" was experienced most strongly by Australia, Canada, and the U.S. This will affect recruiting again as large numbers of "boomers" retire over the next decade. Low fertility rates affect the population growth rates of virtually all Western nations, thus reducing the size of the home-grown recruiting population. The multicultural diversity evident in most Western nations changes the assumptions about the nature of the recruitment pool, especially in those nations that have established distinctly inclusive macro-social diversity policies.

Canada is unique in at least two respects, however. First, it is "the world's only sovereign federation that formally recognizes a national minority (francophone Canadians), ethnic/visible minorities, and aboriginal peoples", in its Constitution and under the Multiculturalism Act. Second, Canada's fertility rate (number of live births per 1,000 population) is the lowest among post-modern states, well below population replacement. Thus, Canada depends heavily on immigration just to maintain its population, which further increases the potential for even greater population diversity. Moreover, the Canadian demographic landscape and the nature of the labour force are changed by the fact that the immigration pattern of the past several decades increasingly favours visible minorities.

In his description of the recruiting context, Leuprecht indicates that recruiting from the traditional pool was greatly influenced by macro-economic conditions and unemployment rates. These do not seem to apply to all cultural groups, particularly aboriginals. This suggests other barriers to raising participation rates among ethno-cultural minorities. The chapter includes a substantial amount of tabulated data on each of the groups designated for systematic attention under the CF's 1999 Employment Equity Plan – women (who have received the highest priority), visible minorities, and aboriginals. In general, these designated groups are vastly under-represented in the CF population, while francophone males (a national minority) are well represented in the CF (in fact, due to their decreasing proportion of the Canadian population, francophones are being over-recruited). Aboriginals and visible minorities are the fastest-growing segments of the Canadian population, while the growth of Caucasian male (the traditional source of CF volunteers) and female segments is stagnant. Although women have made substantial gains in military participation over the past three decades, they are still well below the 28 percent target set by the military in 1999. Also, with respect to aboriginals, Leuprecht observes that the CF attracts more "non-status" than "status" Indians, even though the latter are in the fast-growing majority.

Two options are recommended to ease CF recruitment and retention problems: greater concentration on the traditional sources of personnel (Caucasian males from rural and low-economic-growth areas); or diversity recruitment, with emphasis on recruiting men and women from the ethno-cultural and aboriginal communities. The first option has very little demographic support and would leave the CF vulnerable to higher costs and personnel shortages. Demographic and labour-force trends argue for the diversity strategy that the CF adopted in 1999; while it may have higher resource costs at the outset, it should have substantial pay-off in the longer term. Leuprecht also argues for a diversity approach that places less specific emphasis on women's participation, which he considers to be relatively successful, and a more even approach that focuses intensely on both women and men in all ethno-cultural groups.

Chapter Six

Here, Kathleen MacLaurin focuses specifically on aboriginals, one of Canada's designated groups under the *Employment Equity Act* of 1995, and provides some clues as to why they remain under-represented in the CF. She "seeks to highlight some of the value differences and similarities between the aboriginal (or indigenous) community and those of the military." MacLaurin believes that military leaders must understand the values of aboriginal communities so that they can better deal with those aboriginals who are potential or current CF participants. She notes that values are socially constructed sets of ideals that may vary from one society or person to another. Values are related to our understanding of reality and to what we consider ideal conduct or behaviour within society. Canadians of European descent tend to foster values that determine social conduct, while aboriginal communities tend to cultivate those values that emphasize a "balanced" life.

MacLaurin argues that contemporary aboriginal values have evolved from their "tumultuous" historical past, during which the aboriginal population was reduced by about 90 percent through warfare, disease, starvation and other forms of deprivation after the arrival of white Europeans. They were geographically uprooted and isolated; their lands were taken away and occupied by white people, and they were placed on reservations; their traditional cultures, religions, languages, and associated norms, values, and beliefs, were weakened by these settlers and missionaries, whose descendants perpetuated the damage. While exploitation and marginalization of aboriginals still continue, these communities are slowly recovering their cultural, linguistic, religious, and value heritage, with cultural and social values exhibited by members of aboriginal communities now reflecting both indigenous and European-Canadian influences. Successful human resource planning must acknowledge incompatibilities between aboriginal and military cultural and social value frameworks, as well as identify potential areas of conflict that might obstruct recruitment and retention of aboriginals. Areas of potential conflict, tension and discord, based on differing value orientations, include the following: aboriginal people have a "circular" conception of existence that is consensual in nature, while the military has a "triangular", pyramidal/hierarchical one based on unequal status/power relationships and top-down direction; aboriginals consider all life forms equal, and deference patterns are based on universal respect rather than the unequal social make-up that is the basis for military authority and deference patterns; aboriginals have an ethic of non-interference, which emphasizes "true freedom", discourages interference in the rights, privileges, and activities of others, and precludes any "forced advice", meanwhile the military institution is built upon the superior's imposition of guidance and orders on others.

There are, however, areas of potential compatibility between aboriginal value orientations and those espoused by the CF. For example, on the spiritual level, there is a widespread belief in a "creator" or "higher being." There is also a shared emphasis on collective/team effort and achievement. Both groups place a high value on deliberate socialization (formal or informal) to shape identity, to inculcate acceptable conduct and behavioural norms, and to impart specific skills and cultural knowledge to ensure capable role performance by members. Similarly, there is a common value placed on storytelling as a means of transmitting information and tradition, providing tacit guidance, and establishing personal and competent authority and trust. Finally, there is a mutual value placed on having a self-contained, community medical/health services and professionals, and both groups acknowledge the importance of discipline, honour, and tradition.

Fundamental military policies and practices can often conflict with aboriginal value orientations, and these can further differ among aboriginal groups themselves. Some, for example, acknowledge the Queen as monarch and are willing to accept the "Queen's Commission" and swear an Oath of Allegiance to the Crown. Others reject the monarch and identify more closely with the nation. This would represent a value conflict for those who want to join the military in Canada but not for those interested in the US forces (which some do join). There is also a conflict between some of the family policies, which are based on the nuclear family concept, and aboriginals' emphasis on the extended family, especially in those culture groups where all living relatives, and even some community non-relatives, are considered to be parents or siblings. "The aboriginal individual is the child of the entire community, especially during times of grieving."

Compensation, benefits, and allowances, which are based on a Southern Canadian perspective, do not take account of, for example, what "isolation" may mean for a Northern Canadian native. That a continuous attachment to, and contact with, home and community are likely to be of greater importance to the emotional well-being of aboriginals than to that of most other CF members may need to be reflected in leave and allowance policies.

Moreover, complaint systems may not work as well for aboriginals as they do for non-aboriginals, simply because many aboriginals have been socialized within their culture to not criticize or interfere with others. For example, in conflict or harassment situations, they often report feeling unsupported, misunderstood, or alone when non-aboriginal harassment advisors and other types of "social helpers" are involved. Also, aboriginals often depend on "elders" to provide spiritual support; but the appointment of one "base elder" is unlikely to meet the needs of all aboriginal members. All of these differences indicate a need for policy changes to better accommodate aboriginal members' cultural value obligations. This is unlikely to be an easy task, given the range of ethno-cultural groups that may have claims to cultural or social value differences within the CF.

The chapter concludes with reference to values and the military ethos, the latter having been developed to provide members with the moral basis for service in the CF, among other things. The four core components of the military ethos – warrior/fighting spirit, ethical values, military values, and a reflection of Canadian society – may be interpreted by aboriginals as a form of assimilation or value orientaton suppression. The ethos may thus deter military participation. While this is an important consideration for policy and doctrine, MacLaurin believes the military must maintain its "vital ground" in value orientation to ensure that operational integrity and effectiveness are not compromised. It is the CF's duty to create a values-based workplace that challenges misconceptions of aboriginal peoples and ensures them their rightful place in the military. In this regard, value issues must be understood from an aboriginal perspective for purposes of diversity management. More generally, however, what needs to be determined is the degree to which the reinforcement of the values and identities of any given cultural group might actually work to strengthen force cohesion or, alternately, the point at which such reinforcement might in fact act to reduce force cohesion or mitigate operational effectiveness.

Chapter Seven

This concluding chapter comments briefly on the volume's recurrent themes, and also highlights a number of issues that have not been raised by the other authors. It emphasizes the fact that concepts related to both adaptation (social imperatives) of and resistance (operational imperatives) to encompassing societal "heterogeneity" have existed since at least the 1950s and 1960s, in the work of Morris Janowitz and Samuel Huntington. Ever since, these ideas have been found in oppositional developmental models, but have been overtaken by the diversity model of military participation. Consistent with the gender-diversity approach of Harries-Jenkins, diversity management (both gender and ethno-cultural) may be viewed from this evolutionary historical perspective.

The chapter also emphasizes the conditions that appear necessary to developing an effective diversity-management regime while recognizing that nations and their militaries differ in their perceptions of the need to take an active, positive approach to the issue. Both progressive national legislation and involved, enlightened military leadership are important to the promotion of successful diversity management. Together, these influences tend to move the military toward policies, programs and practices that are more inclusionary (i.e., those necessary to both encompass and accommodate societal diversity). An inclusive military model, one that accepts and attempts to accommodate diversity, will have associated costs, such as increased complexity and the additional effort required to integrate various social and cultural groups. These costs are weighed against the significant benefits: for example, greater social and cultural representation of the population and labour force (for reasons of legitimacy and cost of maintaining quantity and quality levels); greater flexibility in cross-cultural operations; and a likely increased complexity and the additional effort required to integrate various social and cultural groups. These costs are weighed against the significant benefits: for example, greater social and cultural representation of the population and labour force (for reasons of legitimacy and cost of maintaining quantity and quality levels); greater flexibility in cross-cultural operations; and a likely increase in the levels of innovation and creativity in the military workforce.

Finally, there is the question of whether the conceptual perspectives on gender, and the policies and practices that flow from them, have been sufficient to the task of making gender diversity work. In particular, a "fourth option", aimed at achieving a gender-diversity regime (one devoted to uncovering aspects of the current structures, processes, policies, and practices that are "oppressive" to most women and some men) is suggested by the literature on non-military organizational change and development, and by models being developed within some military systems. These bear further consideration by military analysts and policy-makers alike.

NOTES

1   Charles Moskos, "Diversity in the Armed Forces of the United States," in Söeters and van der Meulen, *Managing Diversity in the Armed Forces*: 13-32.

2   Nan Weiner, *Making Cultural Diversity Work* (Scarborough, ON: Carswell, 1997).

3   For a global review of women's participation patterns, see Azura Omar and Marilyn Davidson, "Women in Management: A comparative Cross-Cultural Review", *Journal of International Management*, Vol. 8, No. 2: 35-67.

4   For examples in militaries of the West, see Gwyn Harries-Jenkins, ed., *The Extended Role of Women in Armed Forces*, CRMI Report (Hull: University of Hull, 2002).

5   Weiner, *Making Cultural Diversity Work*, 5-7.

6   For the controversies surrounding the various forms of diversity in nine countries, see, for example, Joseph Söeters and Jan van der Meulen, eds., *Managing Diversity in the Armed Forces* (Amsterdam: Tilburg University Press, 1999).

7   See Chapter 2.

INSTITUTION TO OCCUPATION
TO DIVERSITY:
GENDER IN THE MILITARY TODAY

GWYN HARRIES-JENKINS

INTRODUCTION

A sometimes overlooked feature of the Institutional/Occupational thesis formulated by Moskos[1] is the extent to which the associated models truly represent a sequential development of personnel policies in the military. Simplistically, the traditional *Institutional* model reflects, in this specific context, a custodial management style in which the paternalistic organization "looks after" its personnel.[2] From the 1960s onwards, the difficulties associated with the continuation of a custodial style of management in armed forces became very apparent. Revised military personnel policies consequently reflected to a large extent the argument that supply and demand, rather than normative considerations, were to be paramount.[3] They also accepted the conclusion that the *Occupational* thesis implied priorities of self-interest, rather than those of the military organization *per se*.[4]

Some twenty-five years after the initial formulation of the *Institutional/Occupational* model, contemporary personnel policies in western armed forces are again under critical review. Broadly speaking, there are two primary reasons for this. First, a persistent shortage of personnel, particularly those possessing scarce technical skills, causes major problems of overstretch. The need to provide operationally effective forces capable of responding to new challenges – *the functional imperative* – encourages the consideration of alternative personnel policies. Second, the logic of the business case is matched by a demand for equity. This is in response to socio-legal pressures to widen employment opportunities in the military for hitherto excluded groups.[5] Increasingly, we encounter evidence of demands for the extension to the military of those principles of equal opportunity that are the norm in other organizations. The example of the wider participation of women in the national labour force encourages a review of military personnel policies. Legal decisions that oblige armed forces to recruit and retain such previously excluded groups as gays and lesbians complement legal bans on racial discrimination. The overall effect of these and comparable pressures is that personnel policies in the contemporary Western military have been designed to respond to the needs of a sophisticated *Diversity* thesis. A primary characteristic of this, and of the associated ideal-type model, is succinctly summarized in a 1997 policy letter issued by the Under-Secretary for Personnel of the Dutch Ministry of Defence: "Diversity in gender, age, ethnicity, sexual preference and religion, can be seen as a source of quality for society as a whole."[6]

Diversity in Gender

As Söeters and van der Meulen have shown, successful gender integration in the military is an aspect of the wider search for the effective management of diversity.[7] An important feature of the latter is the provision within the armed forces of pertinent personnel policies that are innately flexible and responsive to changes in the parent society. Two aspects of the *diversity thesis* merit further consideration: the analysis of macro-level personnel policies, and the identification of appropriate personnel policies at the micro level.

At the macro level, it is evident that, over the past thirty years, women have come to play an increasingly important part in Western armed forces.[8] Initially, in the process of opening up the military to women, the primary issue was the identification of the potential role of women in these forces. Subsequently, the traditional policies that excluded women from certain specialties were critically reviewed.[9] Today, contemporary personnel policies in Western armed forces reflect the shift from the traditional exclusion of women from all or some occupational specialties, through qualified inclusion, to open policies of total inclusion. At the same time, the status of women, in terms of recruitment and employ-ment, varies materially in different countries. Thus, Nielsen notes:

> each military has its own history, traditions and culture and the degree of integration of women varies from one to another. Although women have served in armed forces for many years, the debate about the feminization of the military continues, even in countries that are farther down the road of integration than others: about how and where women should serve and train, about the extent to which women should be integrated and even about whether the process has already gone too far. [10]

The sequential development of personnel policies that have been both a cause and an effect of this diversity can be initially analyzed against the typology of roles, as shown in Figure 1.

STAGE	CATEGORY	EXAMPLES
1	Non-Combatant	Military Nurse
2	Combat Service	Clerk; Cook
3	Combat Support	Instrument Fitter; Radar Operator
4	Combat	Pilot; Weapons Operator
5	Direct Ground Combat	Tank Crew; Infanteer
6	Special Operational Forces	Marine Commando; Ranger; SAS

FIGURE 1-1. THE CHANGING ROLES OF WOMEN IN ARMED FORCES

The developmental stages in Figure 1 are not mutually exclusive: there is considerable overlap. Even so, there is ample evidence of a pattern of sequential change. In Stage One, women were formally limited to serving in a non-combatant role, notably nursing. British experience in this area is illustrative of more general military practice. Following the establishment in 1856 of the first purpose-built military hospital staffed by civilian nurses, the Army Nursing Service was set up. More recently, this occupational specialty has been expanded so that today these non-combatant roles include medicine and "specialties allied to medicine". There is, however, throughout the West a continuing tendency in the case of women personnel to identify them primarily with their traditional medical role of military nurse. Irrespective of the uniqueness of their status under the Geneva Convention, nurses in Western armed forces, particularly battlefield specialists, require personal qualities very reminiscent of those attributed to the combat troops: "strength, psychological and emotional stability, bravery under fire and willingness to risk capture".[11]   Paradoxically, in a reversal of common problems of gender integration within the military, a universal contemporary difficulty in Western armed forces is the assimilation of male nurses into a hitherto single-gender environment.

During the First World War, major shortages of male personnel in those countries that had suffered very heavy casualty rates resulted in the recruitment of women to combat service roles. Initially, a cultural legacy was reflected in a considerable reluctance to employ women in other than traditional non-combatant roles. The success, however, of women in non-traditional civilian occupations, such as the munitions industry, encouraged the Western military establishment to reconsider former policies. In April 1915 in Britain, for example, an Army Council Instruction authorized the employment of women as uniformed cooks and waitresses in home-based military establishments. When the Women's Legion received official recognition in February 1916, some of the 6,000 women who were recruited by the end of the year served with the Royal Flying Corps. Here, their occupational specialties were not limited to the traditional women's tasks of clerk and cook, for they also included new technical roles such as motorcycle dispatch rider. This latter role in the French Army was more usually associated with the specialty of *automobiliste* (driver).

From the Second World War onwards, women have been recruited to combat support roles. The history of their role has tended to concentrate on their employment in such visible areas as anti-aircraft batteries and operations rooms. In reality, most served in conventional and mundane roles in communications and logistics occupational specialties. Increasingly, however, military establishments, today, are seeking to make greater use of the ability that women have displayed in these roles. Particular attention is paid to utilizing the intellectual ability, technical skills, and manual dexterity that women have displayed. The majority of women in the Western military today continue to serve in combat service and combat support military occupational specialties. In Belgium, for example, where women constitute 7.3 percent of the total officer corps, some 80 officers in the army serve in combat service and combat support roles, compared with only 12 in the actual combat arms units. In the Air Force, of 65 officers, there is only one female pilot (F-16), although she is not now flying in a combat squadron but is a flight instructor.[12] Nevertheless, personnel policy in Belgium, as elsewhere in the West, continues to encourage women to fill combat roles.

Today, the distinction between combat support and combat roles is less clear than previously. A number of studies have linked this to the changing nature of contemporary warfare.[13] Nevertheless, combat roles *per se* continue to be the core specialties of contemporary armed forces, a status that is reflected in the universal requirement for the most senior military officers to have satisfied the ideal career profile by having served in these specialties.

For women in contemporary armed forces, service in these Stage 4 roles is most readily associated with "impersonal" or "distant" combat. Such roles include aircrew specialties, missile launch operators, and a comprehensive range of billets on board ships. Women serving as aircrew in Afghanistan and on board ships in combat zones would seem to be truly involved in "combat". Even so, for the purpose of analysis, these roles can be distinguished from "direct combat on the ground" specialties, which are to be identified with "units that engage the enemy with individual or crew weapons and with a high probability of physical contact." Practically, these are such specialties as tank crews or infanteers, roles to which women are increasingly recruited in the West. Specific personnel policies, however, are often a reflection of history and national experience. Notwithstanding, for example, the contribution made by women in Russia from 1941-45 when, apart from their role as Partisans, they fought in an all-woman rifle brigade and as tank crews in the Kursk battle[15], they did not, after 1945, serve in Soviet direct ground combat specialties. Conversely, the Canadian decisions of 1982 (*Charter of Rights and Freedoms*) and 1985 (*Canadian Human Rights Act*), together with the Swedish decision of 1989, to open these ground combat specialties to women, reflect a trend away from decisions based on, or affected by, experience to ones determined by legal requirements.

Nevertheless, no women currently serve in combat specialties within special operations forces. These roles are highly distinctive, for such forces differ from conventional military formations in many respects. Two sub-types of non-standard forces can be identified. The first group, operating in a light infantry role, includes Marines, Commandos, Rangers, and Airborne. The second group comprises the even more specialized units of the Special Air Service (SAS), the Special Boat Service (SBS), the SEALS, and the Foreign Legions of some European countries. A distinguishing feature is their principle of interoperability, most readily summarized in the maximum of the United States Marines: "Every man a rifleman". The principle, which was endorsed in the British legal case, *Sirdar v The Army Board*,[16] recognizes the rigours of the environment within which such forces operate. Since individual units or detachments cannot be readily reinforced when casualties are suffered, it is essential that all personnel, irrespective of their secondary occupational specialties, will fight in the primary role of combat soldier. It is the need to maintain this principle that forms the justification for excluding women from combat specialties, although they may serve in combat service, combat support, or combat at a distance roles, as in the US Marines.

Policy Differences

Further analysis suggests that diversity in gender is reflected not only in the typology of changing roles, but also in the specific policies that are adopted in various countries. Distinctive patterns of inclusion/exclusion policies contribute to this diversity: total exclusion, partial exclusion, partial inclusion, or total inclusion.

In Western armed forces, personnel policies that lead to the total exclusion of women are now increasingly a thing of the past. They were until recently, however, exemplified by the situation in Turkey and Italy. In the former, a change of policy in 1960 excluded women from military education; no female cadets were allowed in military schools until 1992. Today, Turkish servicewomen, who number 917 (0.1 percent of total force strength), can serve only as officers and are excluded from direct combat on the ground roles, as well as from submarines. By 1999 Italy was the only NATO military that excluded women altogether. The pressure group *La Associazone Nationale Aspirante Donne Soldato* (The Association of Aspiring Women Soldiers) campaigned for many years for a change in official policy. Eventually, in September 1999, the Italian Parliament agreed to allow women to serve in the military; and there are now 438 women (0.1 percent of the total force strength) who serve, mainly in combat service and combat support posts.

In Germany, the policy of partial exclusion was, until 2000, laid down in the *Soldatengesetz* (German Law on Soldiers) and Article 3a of the *Soldatenlaufbahnverordnung* (Regulation on Soldiers' Careers). The latter, in particular, decreed that women could enlist only as volunteers and only in the medical and military music services (i.e., bands). The law was challenged by Tanya Kreil, an electronics specialist, who applied in 1996 to serve in the Bundeswehr as a volunteer. When her request was turned down, she argued that the rejection of her application on the sole basis of her gender was contrary to European Community Law. This was upheld by the Court of Justice of the European Community.[17] All posts in the Bundeswehr were subsquently opened to women. In October 2001, there were 6,503 women in the German armed forces (3.4 percent of total force strength), and the long-term target is 15,000 women (5.3 percent) in a future standing strength of 289,000.[18]

By contrast, the United Kingdom currently (2002) maintains a strict policy of partial inclusion. This means that while more than 95 percent of posts in the air force, together with 70 percent of posts in both the navy and army, are open to women, specific restrictions on their extended employment still apply. These essentially relate to those occupational specialties where the primary duty is "to close with and kill the enemy",[19] or where problems of privacy or occupational health prevail. The logic of this policy is consistently challenged. A persistent argument notes that the number of direct combat on the ground posts in the contemporary Army is small, reflecting a long-term trend for their decline over time.[20] The conclusion that a policy of partial inclusion is, therefore, no longer empirically satisfied is reinforced by the contention that the changing operational functions of the military and developments in weapons technology no longer logically justify exclusion.

The total inclusion of gender-neutral armed forces is most readily demonstrated in those continental European countries that have adopted specific personnel policies to this end. The Nordic countries, for example, are in many respects the most progressive countries in this regard. In 1985, Norway became the first in NATO to allow women to serve in all combat functions, including service in submarines. Denmark adopted a policy of total inclusion in 1988. Canadian servicewomen have been able to serve in almost all occupational specialties since 1989. The remaining restriction – on their serving aboard submarines – was lifted in March 2001. In theory, all positions are open to women in both the Dutch and French militaries. The distinction here between policy and practice, however, has to be carefully noted. In both the Netherlands and France, for instance, access to some occupational specialties is, in reality, restricted, usually on the grounds of physical requirements, combat effectiveness, or the health problems associated with submarine service. Portuguese servicewomen can also, in theory, apply for all posts, but in practice, service in the marines and other combat specialties remains closed to the 2,875 female personnel. A similar situation exists in Spain where, although most specialties are open to women, including combat roles, more than 50 percent of the 6,462 servicewomen serve in combat service and combat support posts.

Micro-Level Personnel Policies

While the basic characteristics of the diversity model can be seen in the changing roles of women in the military and in different national macro-level policies and practices, it is the micro-level personnel policies that most readily reflect the defining characteristics of the model. The traditional institutional and occupational models of armed forces begin from the premise, implicit or explicit, that the ideal military image is that of the physically strong, emotionally tough, masculine war hero. Typified by The American Enlisted Man[21] and Squaddies,[22] this is the dominant "ideal-type".[23] It encompasses what Dunivin terms, "the combat masculine war-fighting (CMW) paradigm".[24] The associated military culture is seen to be, for it is largely shaped and determined by men.[25] In contrast, the diversity model starts from the fundamental premise that the organization, structure, and management of the military reflect the norms and values of civilian society. The heterogeneous nature of the latter is reflected in armed forces in an inclusionary ideal-type image, which is created and reinforced by the adopted micro-level personnel policies.

This image is a corollary of the development of the "post-modern military", a defining characteristic of which is the recognition of gender diversity. There is a shift from policies of segregation or the exclusion of women toward their greater integration into the armed forces. Unlike the institutional and occupational models, which require individuals to adapt to the fixed values of the military – the "adaptative" thesis – the diversity model is based on the acceptance of differences. The model is, accordingly, the antithesis of the combat, masculine, war-fighting image, for it is driven by demands for inclusiveness and heterogeneity, rather than by the CMW traditions of exclusiveness and homogeneity.[26]

The relationship of these micro-level personnel policies to the establishment of a diversity model that reflects a demand for mutual accommodation is, however, noticeably complex. A consistent issue is the difficulty of reconciling the primary objective of effective impartial, mixed-gender social and operational integration with the demand to recognize and accommodate the special needs of women soldiers. The primary objective is conventionally identified with the concept of gender-neutrality, which is a significant characteristic of the post-modern military.[27] The specific needs of women soldiers, on the other hand, are seen to be very significant, albeit that many of the more contentious micro-level policies, such as paid parental leave, actually apply to all personnel, irrespective of gender.

The required balance is one in which the agreed policies implement equal opportunities legislation while allowing for the maintenance of a military system that ensures combat capability. This means optimizing "the richness of individual diversity that is available".[28] To achieve this, personnel policies at the micro-level have to take into consideration three specific issues: tokenism, equal opportunities, and positive discrimination.

Tokenism

Consistently, micro-level personnel policies demonstrate their concern with tokenism. Notwithstanding the opening-up of a greater number and variety of occupational specialties to women, they continue to be under-represented in contemporary armed forces. Very little appears to have changed since Enloe drew attention to the issues in this context.[29] Among the human resources management (HRM) problems to which this under-representation gives rise, that of tokenism is most prominent. This follows from the imperfect male-female ratio in most military occupational specialties. According to Kanter, the problem of tokenism arises when the male/female ratio for personnel is below 85/15.[30] For the status of women in armed forces to approach that of a minority population, the ratio has to be at least 65/35. Notwithstanding the increased recruitment of women to the armed forces over the last thirty years, the ratio between male and female personnel continues to be well below that of the ratio in society as a whole. Rarely does the proportion of women in the military approach Kanter's 15 percent minimum (the United States comes close at 14.0 percent and New Zealand even closer at 14.5 percent), let alone exceed this (as Australia does, at 16.8 percent). The situation in a selection of Western armed forces is given in Figure Two.

COUNTRY	TOTAL POP	POP AGE 18-32	FEMALE POP AGE 18-32		TOTAL ACTIVE ARMED FORCES	ACTIVE WOMEN PERSONNEL	
THOUSANDS				%	NUMBER	NUMBER	%
Belgium	10,126	1,987	977	49.2	41,428	3,190	7.7
Canada	29,512	5,990	2,955	49.3	57,526	6,558	11.4
Denmark	5,267	1,051	517	49.2	15,409	863	5.6
France	59,425	12,223	5,982	48.9	323,717	27,516	8.5
Germany	82,112	16,568	8,040	48.5	200,821	5,623	2.8
Greece	10,692	2,358	1,151	48.8	161,973	6,155	3.8
Italy	57,930	12,182	5,375	44.1	250,600	438	0.17
Netherlands	15,794	3,104	1,512	48.7	52,125	4,170	8.0
Norway	4,443	911	442	48.5	36,000	1,152	3.2
Spain	39,237	9,364	4,564	48.7	111,414	6,462	5.8
UK	58,882	11,528	5,637	48.8	205,222	16,623	8.1
US	275,636	56,102	27,614	49.2	1,417,514	198,452	14.0

SOURCES: CALCULATED FROM *ANNUAL REVIEW OF WOMEN IN NATO'S ARMED FORCES 2000-2001*; IISS, THE MILITARY BALANCE, 2000-2001 (OXFORD: OXFORD UNIVERSITY PRESS, 2000) AND NATIONAL MOD STATISTICS.

FIGURE 2.   REPRESENTATION OF WOMEN IN SELECTED WESTERN ARMED FORCES

Accordingly, women in the contemporary military do not form even a minority population. If, within the diversity model, women are quantitatively to reflect their numerical distribution in the population at large – that is, almost 50 percent of the 18-32-age cohort in the total population – then positive recruiting policies and strategies have to be adopted. Coincidentally, if these are to be effective, they must reflect those policies that represent the best practice in major organizations within civil society as well as in military systems in general.

At the same time, some personnel policies, particularly in the area of recruitment, can have dysfunctional consequences, irrespective of their basic objective of reducing tokenism. The considerable publicity, for example, given to an English-educated female F-14 pilot serving in the Afghan theatre exemplifies this. This publicity considerably damaged the claims of other women filling combat roles to be seen as full members of a mixed-gender team. Women serving in operational theatres have consistently reacted to attempts to publicize their individual roles, rather than their gender-neutral contribution to the effectiveness of an integrated team. Additionally, as O'Neill comments, too much discussion of the role of women in the integrated military "has centred on a few highly publicized incidents". [31]

The dynamics of tokenism consistently affect the status of women in the diversity model. According to the 1997 RAND study, both officers and senior enlisted personnel felt that publicity such as that given to individual women like Captain Linda Bray in 1989 during *Operation Just Cause in Panama*, "causes problems within the military where none may otherwise exist". The study draws particular attention to the response of one interviewee that, "the more they do things like this, the more they set us apart". [32] Nevertheless, women continue to be highly visible as members of what is, at best, a minority group. Social control by the dominant majority group of men continues to be intensive in its demands for the conformity of the minority group to the norms and values of the majority. [33] One consequence of this is the growing sense of acute work stress. Bray et al. suggest that,

> The nature of such stress and the underlying factors contributing to it…may be a result of particular features of military life, the challenges of competing in a predominantly male organization…problems of unwanted sexual advances or harassment by their male counterparts, the result of relatively poor coping skills, or some combination of these or other factors. [34]

Equal Opportunities

A further significant characteristic of the diversity model is the need to adapt HRM policies to encourage the enhanced recruitment and retention of women in armed forces. This is exemplified by Dutch experience.[35] Against a current proportion of 8 percent women in the total military force, the 2010 target is 12 percent, even though this is still below the critical mass of 20 to 25 percent specified by Kanter. Even to achieve this lower target micro-level personnel policies are required in the Netherlands that recognize the difficulties faced by women in the military who seek to combine a career with raising a family. One answer to this is the provision of policies which provide for, *inter alia*, paid parental leave, on-base childcare, flexible working hours, part-time work, and guaranteed re-entry rights after maternity leave.

Such policies closely resemble those that are the norm in civilian organizations, where they not only meet the needs of equal opportunities legislation but also ensure the provision of effective recruitment and retention strategies. Their critics, however, remind us that this "favourable" treatment of a minority contradicts the armed forces' traditional insistence on the principle of equal treatment of all individuals within the rules and regulations of a military code of justice.

Equally, it is argued that the differential treatment of individuals, or a group, weakens a basic feature of the military as a crisis organization. In common with similar organizations, such as the ambulance service, fire brigade, hospitals, and the police, armed forces exist to provide operational effectiveness 24 hours a day, 365 days a year. "Effectiveness" presumes that all personnel are available, as and when required. As van der Meulen notes, "You can't possibly be a part-time soldier in Kosovo (or Afghanistan)." [36]

The underlying reasons are seen in the discussions in the *Sirdar* case. Given the importance to the military, as a crisis organization, of immediate and total operational effectiveness, two questions arise: can this be ensured without the whole-hearted and full commitment of all personnel, and does the non-availability of the latter, irrespective of their gender, fundamentally weaken the ability of armed forces to meet their operational goals?

Effectively, however, the successful resolution of these questions is largely a matter of HRM policy and practice. Canadian experience in this context accordingly argues that gender diversity does not detract from operational effectiveness: "There need not be a manning shortfall for a unit if a member becomes pregnant." [37]

In the past, many manning shortfalls arising from such factors as sickness, leave, detachments, and training schedules were avoided through the presence of personnel "held above establishment". Filling key positions was always more difficult, although strategies such as "acting up", "personnel substitution", and more general policies of "interoperability" were helpful. In the contemporary military, however, a leaner establishment often precludes the retention of extra or surplus personnel, while the increasing demands of specialist military technology limit the use of substitution or interoperability strategies. Accordingly, one of the characteristic features of micro-level personnel policies in the diversity model is the constant preoccupation with the need to balance the requirements of equal opportunities legislation with the functional requirements of the effective armed force.

Positive Discrimination

In discussions of the role and status of women in the post-modern military, a common observation is the under-representation of women in senior ranks at both officer and non-commissioned officer levels. For the United Kingdom, evidence given to the Defence Committee in 2001 illustrates this (see Figure 3).

YEAR	ROYAL NAVY			ARMY			ROYAL AIR FORCE		TOTAL FEMALE STRENGTH
	N	CAPT	C'DORE	N	COL	BRIG	N	AIR C'DORE	ALL SERVICES
1997	439	3	0	1,062	8	0	879	2	14,831
2000	517	4	0	1,279	-	1	1,095	1	16,547
2001	561	-	1	1,317	-	3	1,155	0	16,686

NUMBER: TOTAL NUMBER OF WOMEN OFFICERS.
SOURCE: EVIDENCE TO DEFENCE COMMITTEE, 2001, AND DEFENCE ANALYTICAL SERVICES AGENCY (DASA).

FIGURE 3. SENIOR FEMALE OFFICERS: SELECTED YEARS

As of 1 October 2001, women constituted 8.1 percent of the total force strength in the United Kingdom, a figure expected to rise to 10 percent by 2006. They constitute some 9.5 percent of all officers in the armed services but continue to be under-represented at the senior officer levels. Similar situations are to be seen elsewhere in European armed forces. In analyzing, for example, the representation of women in the Belgian military, Manigart observes that "it appears that the higher the rank, the fewer women there are".[38] In Belgium, female enlisted personnel (privates) in 2001 comprised 10.1 percent of the force strength at that rank; however, only 5.8 percent of non-commissioned officers and 4.7 percent of officers are women. Moreover, while these percentage figures are increases on previous years, the absolute number of women officers and NCOs does not show a corresponding increase at 236 and 1,017, respectively. Similar conclusions are reached in a study of the integration of women in the Danish military, where they comprise 8 percent of the enlisted personnel, 4 percent of the sergeants, and 3 percent of officers. Only three women from a total strength of 345 serve at the rank of lieutenant colonel (0.9 percent).[39]

A critical issue when reviewing this under-representation of women at these rank levels, is whether specific HRM strategies are required that would change these force profiles. Such strategies, in overcoming the unique problems faced by woman soldiers, are to be identified with policies of positive discrimination. A number of reasons can be advanced to rationalize the latter: convergence with civilian working practice, establishment of role models, image building, and cultural change. [40]

Whereas the institutional model of the military reflects a divergence perspective, in which armed forces are seen to be different from other complex organizations, both the occupational and diversity models represent convergence. This is particularly noticeable in the latter case, where a basic characteristic of the diversity model is the extent to which the military follows very closely the policies and practices of organizations in the parent society as these affect minority and hitherto excluded groups. In terms of gender diversity, this convergence suggests that, to be successful, micro-level personnel policies should follow civilian practice and discriminate in favour of women personnel.

An initial question is that of promotion. Under-representation at the noted rank levels invites revised promotion strategies that resemble more closely those adopted in civil organizations. Increasingly, women are being promoted in these organizations at younger ages. The governing personnel policies reflect a preference for using professional ability and pertinent experience as criteria for promotion, rather than relying on the more impersonal and objective criteria of age and seniority. Extending these policies to armed forces, however, raises a number of critical issues. First, military organizations in peace time have consistently projected an image of the ideal career profile as linking age and seniority to a particular rank. Deviations from the norm are seen to recognize exceptional professional ability (the institutional model) or skill shortages (the occupational model). In the diversity model, however, deviations from the standard rules and regulations reflect the wish to recognize the specific needs of particular sub-groups. This contradicts basic defining criteria of the status of the military as a bureaucratized profession or a professionalized bureaucracy.[41] One such criterion specifies that in the pure type of legal authority, the "office", "[It] constitutes a career. There is a system of 'promotion' according to seniority or to achievement, or both. Promotion is dependent on the judgement of superiors." [42]

This summary of promotion policies in the institutional model contrasts markedly with the expectation in the diversity model that the sub-group – in this case, women – should receive favoured treatment. Where this is not forthcoming, those who are dissatisfied may take as their reference group their professional counterparts in civilian organizations. Subsequent comparisons may result in a sense of relative deprivation that, whether or not it is actual, can adversely affect individual morale and motivation. This is particularly evident where comparison with the reference group is a part of a more general preference for cosmopolitan rather than local relationships. Indeed, a significant characteristic of the diversity military thesis, in contrast with that of the institutional model, is this identification on the part of individuals with cosmopolitan values. Yet promotional policies that are differentiated so as to minimize any sense of deprivation or dissatisfaction will always generate resentment among less favoured personnel.

At the same time, effective promotion policies are mandatory if the organization is to produce adequate and sufficient role models who are local rather than cosmopolitan in their attitudes. As noted, there is a general shortage in the Western armed forces of senior women at both the commissioned and the non-commissioned levels. In the latter instance, an exception to the general rule can be seen in France where, of the 27,500 active women personnel who form 8.5 percent of the whole force, 58.5 percent are to be found in senior non-commissioned ranks, compared with 53.5 percent of male personnel. With higher average educational levels than men at the time of joining the French armed forces, women are particularly suited to administrative and technical posts. This is most noticeable in the navy, where the highest concentration of women (72 percent) is to be found among petty officers.[43] Nevertheless, for the small proportion of women in the French military who are officers (5 percent compared with 13 percent for men), the paucity of role models is comparable with the situation to be found elsewhere in the European military.

The earlier discussion of tokenism within the contemporary military noted that publicity given to individual female members of armed forces may be dysfunctional. Yet there continues to be considerable pressure to establish an appropriate image for women service personnel. The underlying problems are complex. For some critics, such an image would be the antithesis of the traditional combat-masculine-warrior (CMW) paradigm. It would also represent a break with the almost exclusively male "Old Military" image identified by Gutmann.[44] In the diversity model, however, three factors are important in image-building. First, an exclusive focus on the norms and ideals associated with masculinity on the one hand or femininity on the other "distorts our understanding of both the military and the whole activity of warfare".[45] An image of the institutional/occupational military as masculine and aggressive cannot simply be replaced in the diversity model by one that is feminine, nurturing, and protective. Second, as we have noted, the institutional imperatives of the military with their concern for rank and authority cannot be pushed to one side on the grounds that they are anachronistic and irrelevant to the diversity model. Finally, any projected image, irrespective of gender, has to incorporate those communal values of the military that differentiate it from other complex, large-scale organizations.

What this means in practice is that the ideal image consistently represents a balance between the "business case" on the one hand and the "equity case" on the other. In this balancing act, women are said to be in a situation that is all too familiar to token and minority group members in a liberal-democratic country:

> Either they bank on equality of treatment as the system encourages them to do, only to discover that the universal rules that govern it were historically designed for men only and still mechanically favour the majority, or they play up their identity, but find that in a traditionally virile culture, there are stigmas attached to it. [46]

The ideal role model, in consequence, continues to be plagued by uncertainty because the image of contemporary armed forces is imperfect and still developing.

This uncertainty is also to be seen in the demand for the provision of micro-level personnel policies that will encourage and ensure cultural change. The concept of the culture of armed forces is complex. An initial difficulty reflects definitional problems, not least because there are said to be some 54 definitions of the terms "organizational culture"[47] Significantly, many of the determining characteristics of that culture – symbolism, rituals, heroes, and core values – were taken for granted in armed forces for many years, prior to the publication of the "new" concept of organizational culture by Pettigrew.[48] In regard to the institutional model of the military, studies in the 1940s linked the concept to the rational symbols, rituals, and values of the bureaucracy.[49] Subsequent studies focussed on features of the occupational model, which implicitly identified the cultural variable with "the way we do things around here".[50] A common feature of these and of the wider studies of the military as a bureaucratized profession and a professionalized bureaucracy[51] was the identification of the culture of armed forces with the prevailing assumptions, norms, values, customs, and traditions that collectively, over time, created a set of shared expectations amongst military personnel.[52] Essentially, however, these reflected the continuance of a predominantly masculine interpretation of a monolithic culture, which uniquely set the military apart from other organizations.

With an increasing percentage of women in the contemporary military, there is evidence within the diversity model of an enhanced demand for the changing of this culture. Events such as *Tailhook* are said to justify such a demand. Recent Canadian studies indicate that women in the combat arms still find themselves in an environment in which the dominant culture encourages their non-acceptance.[53] There is, however, little agreement as to how culture change can best be realized.[54] A preliminary question is whether change can be "top-down". From an integration perspective, this suggests for the military the use of policies comparable with those employed in civil organizations. Widen accordingly suggests that, "The strategic leader should recognise that military cultures exist, that they impact the armed forces, and that they can be managed."[55]

An alternative perspective, which acknowledges the existence within the military organization of a number of sub-cultures, is highly critical of imposed change and its dysfunctional consequences.[56] It is possible to adopt the standpoint that organizational cultures are so heterogeneous that it is impossible to introduce planned change.[57] This *fragmentation* perspective[58] is highly reminiscent of the chaos theory that is said to describe the day-to-day operations of the military organization.[59] A more positive approach, therefore, is required, one that recognizes gender identity as a crucial component of the organizational culture of contemporary armed forces.

Such an approach begins with an acceptance at the macro-level of the legal requirements to adopt policies governing the inclusion of women in the military. Thereafter, micro-level policies are required that accept the role of women in the military to be socially constituted.[60] Since an identifying characteristic of military culture is the presence of "heroes", positive discriminatory promotion policies, that will ensure the emergence of role models are required, at least in the short term. Linked with this is the identification within the diversity model of those unacceptable aspects of contemporary military life that need to be addressed. The overall objective is to facilitate the greater understanding of the permanence and importance of the diversity model of the military while maintaining cohesion and combat effectiveness.

The institutional model of armed forces reflected the innate conservatism of the military man. It was, as Boëne notes, "A true mirror of the larger (male) society, it comprises all the support functions it needs to wage war...."[61] This emphasis on the importance of the functional imperative was continued in the later occupational model proposed by Charles Moskos.[62]   Today, however, not only is the pertinence of conservative, male-dominated anachronistic models questioned, but their very conceptual validity is in doubt. The diversity model argues that, in a situation of free choice within all-volunteer forces, heterogenic influences, and demanded representativeness, the primary functional military objectives of combat effectiveness have to be matched by the acceptance of differences. Inclusiveness and heterogeneity, rather than exclusiveness and homogeneity, have to prevail.

NOTES

1   Charles C. Moskos, "From Institution to Occupation: Trends in military organization," *Armed Forces and Society* 4 (1977): 41-50.

2   Jacques van Doorn, *Organisatie en Maatschappi*, (Leyden: Stenfert Krocse, 1966), 207-26.

3   Charles C. Moskos, "The American Enlisted Man in the All-Volunteer Army," in David R. Segal and H. Wallace Sinaiko, *Life in the Rank and File* (Washington DC: Pergammon-Brassey, 1986), 365-57.

4   See G. Harries-Jenkins and C. Moskos, "Armed Forces and Society: Trend Report," *Current Sociology* 29.3 (Winter 1981); Franklin C. Pinch, "Military Manpower and Social Change," *Armed Forces and Society* 8 (Summer 1982): 575-600; David R. Segal and Mady W. Segal, "Change in Military Organization," *Annual Review of Sociology* 9 (1983): 151-170; Charles C. Moskos, "Institutional/Occupational Trends in Armed Forces: An Update," *Armed*

Forces and Society 12.3 (Spring 1986): 377-382; David R. Segal, "Measuring the Institutional/Occupational Thesis," A*rmed Forces and Society* 12.3 (Spring 1986); G. Caforio, "The Military Profession: Theory of Change," A*rmed Forces and Society* 15.1 (Fall 1998): 55-70; Henning Sørensen, "New Perspectives on the Military Profession," *Armed Forces and Society* 20.4 (Summer 1994): 599-617.

5   Christopher Dandeker and David Mason, "The British Armed Services and the Participation of Minority Ethnic Communities: From Equal Opportunities to Diversity?", *The Sociological Review* (May 2001).

6   Jan van der Meulen, "Slow Integration: Women in the Dutch Military" in *The Extended Role of Women in Armed Forces*, ed. G. Harries-Jenkins, CRMI Report (Hull: University of Hull, 2002).

7   J. Soëters and Jan van der Meulen, eds., *Managing Diversity: Experiences from nine countries*, (Tilberg: Tilberg University Press, 1999).

8   Nancy Goldman, "The Changing Role of Women in the Armed Forces," *American Journal of Sociology* 78 (1973): 892-911.

9   See Brent Scowcroft, ed., *Military Service in the United States* (Englewood Cliffs NJ: Prentice-Hall, 1982); Martha Marsden, "The Continuing Debate: Women Soldiers in the US Army," in *Life in the Rank and File*, eds. David R. Segal and H. Wallace Sinaiko (Washington DC: Pergamon-Brassey, 1986); M. C. Devilbiss, *Women and Military Service: A History, Analysis and Overview of Key Issues* (Maxwell Air Force Base, AL: Air University Press, 1990); Rita James Simon, ed., *Women in the Military*, (New Brunswick, NJ: Transaction Publishers, 2001).

10   Vicky Nielsen, "Women in Uniform," *NATO Review* (Summer 2001): 30.

11   (Fenner, 2001: 11).

12   Philippe Manigart, "The Extended Role of Women in Armed Forces: The Case of Belgium," in *The Extended Role of Women*, Harries-Jenkins.

13   See M. Clarke, ed., *New Perspectives on Security* (London: Brassey, 1993; Segal and Segal, "Change in Military Organization"); Christopher Dandeker, "Policy for People, Problems and Prospects," in *Brassey's Defence Annual* (London: 1999); C. Donnelly, "Shaping Soldiers for the 21st Century," *NATO Review*, 2000; Caroline Kennedy-Pipe, "Women and the Military," *Journal of Strategic Studies* 23.4 (December 2000): 32-50.

14   Les Aspin, "Direct Combat Definition and Assignment Rule," *Memorandum from the Secretary of Defense*, 13 January 1994.

15   See Jean K. Cotton, "Soviet Women in Combat in World War II: The Ground Forces and the Navy," *International Journal of Women's Studies* 3 (1980): 345-357; Mary Buckley, Women and Ideology in the Soviet Union (London: Harvester Wheatsheaf, 1989); Alexievich Svetlana, "I am loath to recall: Russian soldiers in World War II," *Women's Studies Quarterly* 3 and 4 (1995): 78-84.

16   *Sirdar v. The Army Board, Secretary of State for Defence* (ECJ, 1999, C.273/97).

17   *Kreil v Bundesrepublik Deutchsland* (ECJ Case C-285/98).

18   Bernhard Fleckenstein (2002), "Women in the German Armed Forces: They should be all they can be," in Harries-Jenkins, *The Extended Role of Women in Armed Forces*.

19   Nielsen, "Women in Uniform".

20   David H. J. Morgan, "Theatres of War: Combat, the Military and Masculinities" in Harry Brod and Michael Kaufman, eds., *Theorizing Masculinities* (London: Sage,1994), 165-182.

21   Charles C. Moskos, *The American Enlisted Man: The Rank and File in Today's Military* (New York: Russell Sage Foundation, 1970).

22   John Hockey, *Squaddies: Portrait of a Subculture* (Exeter: Exeter University Press, 1986).

23   R. W. Connell, "Masculinity, Violence and War," in Michael Kimmel and Michael Messner, eds., *Men's Lives* (Boston: Alleyn and Bacon, 1995); F. J. Barrett, "The Organization and Construction of Hegemonic Masculinity: The Case of the US Navy," *Gender, Work and Organization* 3 (1996): 129-142.

24   Karen Dunivin, "Military Culture: Change and Continuity," *Armed Forces and Society* 20 (Summer 1994): 531-548.

25   Donna Winslow, "Rites of Passage and Group Bonding in the Canadian Airborne," *Armed Forces and Society* 25.3 (Spring 1999): 429-457.

26   Franklin C. Pinch, "Gender Integration in Elite Ground Combat Units: Selected issues and constraints on full integration in Canada," in Harries-Jenkins, *The Extended Role of Women in Armed Forces.*

27   Charles C. Moskos, John Williams, and David R, Segal, *The Postmodern Military* (Oxford: Oxford University Press, 2000).

28   George Robertson, "Learning from Experience," Transcript of speech to Equal Opportunities Conference of the Ministry of Defence, 10 November 1998.

29   Cynthia Enloe, *Does Khaki Become You? The Militarisation of Women's Lives* (London: South End Press, 1983).

30   Rosabeth Moss Kanter, *Men and Women of the Corporation* (New York: Basic Books, 1977), 208-9.

31   William O'Neill, "Women and Readiness," in *Women in the Military*, Simon, 173.

32   Margaret C. Harrell and Laura L. Miller, *New Opportunities for Military Women: Effects upon Readiness, Cohesion and Morale*, DASWO1-95-C-0059 (Santa Monica: RAND, 1997), 95.

33   Joseph Soëters, "Women as Tokens in the Military," in *The Extended Role of Women in Armed Forces*, Harries-Jenkins.

34   R. M. Bray, C. S. Camlin, J. A. Fairbank, G. H. Dunteman, and S. C. Wheeless, "The effects of stress on job functioning of military men and women," *Armed Forces and Society* 27 (Spring 2001): 411-12.

35   Jan van der Meulen, "Slow Integration: Women in the Dutch Military".

36   Ibid.

37   *Despatches*, "Leadership in a Mixed Gender Environment," Despatches, The Army Lessons Learned Centre 5.2 (1998): 6.

38   Manigart, "The Case of Belgium," in *The Extended Role of Women in Armed Forces*, Harries-Jenkins.

39   Henning Sørensen, "Women in the Danish Armed Forces," in *The Extended Role of Women in Armed Forces*, Harries-Jenkins.

40   Joseph Soëters, "Women as Tokens in the Military," in *The Extended Role of Women in Armed Forces*, Harries-Jenkins.

41   Morris Janowitz, "Changing Patterns of Organizational Authority in the Military Establishment," *Administrative Science Quarterly* III (1959): 474-93.

42   Talcott Parsons, ed., *Max Weber: The Theory of Social and Economic Organization*, New York: The Free Press, 1964), 334.

43   Bernard Boëne, "The Changing Place of Servicewomen Under France's New All-Volunteer Force," in *The Extended Role of Women in Armed Forces*, Harries-Jenkins.

44   Stephanie Gutmann, *The Kinder, Gentler Military: Can America's Gender-Neutral Fighting Force Still Win Wars?* (New York: Scribner, 2000).

45   Regina F. Titunik, "The First Wave: Gender Integration and Military Culture," *Armed Forces and Society* 26.2 (Winter 2000): 229-257.

46   Bernard Boëne, "Western-Type Civil-Military Relations Revisited," in *Military, State and Society in Israel*, Daniel Maman and Eyal Ben-Ari (New Brunswick NJ: Transaction Publishers, 2001).

Bernard, "The Changing Place of Servicewomen Under France's New All-Volunteer Force," in *The Extended Role of Women in Armed Forces*, Harries-Jenkins.

47   W. Verbeke, M. Volgering, and M. Hessels, "Exploring the Conceptual Expansion within the Field of Organizational Behaviour, Organizational Climate and Organizational Culture," *Journal of Management Studies* 35.3 (1998): 315.

48   A. Pettigrew, "On Studying Organizational Cultures," *Administrative Science Quarterly* 24 (1979): 570-81.

49   See Ralph Turner, "The Navy Disbursing Officer as a Bureaucrat," *American Sociological Review* 10 (1947): 60-8; and Arthur K. Davis, "Bureaucratic Patterns in the Navy Office Corps," *Social Forces* 27 (1948): 143-53.

50   See Charles C. Moskos, *The American Enlisted Man: The Rank and File in Today's Military* (New York: Russell Sage Foundation, 1970); Alan Ned Sabrosky, ed., *Blue Collar Soldiers* (Philadelphia: Foreign Policy Research Institute, 1977); and Michel Martin, *Warriors to Managers* (Chapel Hill NC: The University of North Carolina Press, 1981).

51   Harries-Jenkins and Moskos, "Armed Forces and Society: Trend Report".

52   See Dunivin, "Military Culture: Change and Continuity"; James Burk, "Military Culture," in *Encyclopedia of Violence, Peace and Conflict* 2 (New York: Academic Press, 1999); and Donna Winslow, *Army Culture* (Ottawa: Programme for Research on Peace, Security and Society: University of Ottawa, 2001).

53   K. Davis and V. Thomas, *Chief Land Staff Gender Integration Study: The Experience of Women Who Have Served in the Combat Arms*, Sponsor Research Report 98-1 (Ottawa, Department of National Defence Personnel Research Team, 1998),7.

54   D. Druckman, J. E. Singer, and H. Van Cott, eds., *Enhancing Organizational Performance* (Washington DC: National Academy Press, 1997), 7.

55   S. C. Widen, *United States Military Cultures: A Mandatory Lesson for Senior Service College Curriculum* (Carlisle, PA: US Army War College, 1997), 20.

56   Hockey, *Squaddies*.

57   M. Alvesson and P. O. Berg, *Corporate Culture and Organizational Symbolism* (New York: Walter de Gruyter, 1992).

58   Winslow, *Army Culture*.

59   See Norman Dixon, On the Psychology of *Military Incompetence* (London: Random House, 1976); and R. Beaumont, *War, Chaos and History* (London: Praeger, 1994).

60   Mady Wechsler Segal, "Women's military roles cross nationally: past, present and future," *Gender and Society* 9.6 (1995): 757-75.

61   Bernard Boëne, "Western-Type Civil-Military Relations Revisited," in *Military, State and Society in Israel*, Daniel Maman and Eyal Ben-Ari (New Brunswick NJ: Transaction Publishers, 2001), 54.

62   Moskos, "From Institution to Occupation".

WOMEN IN THE MILITARY:
FACING THE WARRIOR FRAMEWORK

KAREN D. DAVIS AND BRIAN MCKEE

INTRODUCTION

In recent decades women have joined the ranks of the military in most Western nations. While initial opposition and resistance appear to have been overcome, there is still debate over the appropriateness of employing women in some military occupations, roles, and areas of expertise. Many nations still do not allow women to serve in combat roles or in submarines. This chapter highlights some of the central concerns—some bordering on myth—regarding the participation of women in the military, and is thereby intended to add some clarification to what has become a prolonged debate. The context of this debate is the general experience of Western nations in expanding the roles and participation of women in their militaries; however, we rely upon the example of Canada to illustrate general trends and themes. We reiterate a message, well argued by others: that the real hurdle for women in participating fully in the military today has little to do with their physical and mental abilities but rather revolves around social and cultural issues characterizing a "warrior" framework. Finally, in identifying those characteristics and abilities that are becoming increasingly necessary within a modern military, we discuss the strategic importance of shifting the focus to relevant research to ensure that credible information informs decision-making with respect to the roles of women in the military.

BACKGROUND

Military policies in Canada and many other Western democracies have reflected the personnel needs of the military organizations, as well as the increasing emphasis on gender equality within those countries. Women in Anglo-American countries (e.g., Australia,

Canada, New Zealand, the United Kingdom, and the United States)
have served in some capacity since the First World War. However,
the real turning point for women came in the 1960s and 1970s,
when various forms of legislation provided for greater equality of
women in the labour force as a whole,[1] and specifically for their
expanded participation in the military.[2] In 1989 in Canada, for
example, a Canadian Human Rights Commission (CHRC) Tribunal
directed that all trials of women in non-traditional roles were to
cease and that women were to be fully integrated into all Canadian
Forces (CF) roles except service on submarines.[3] In 2001, that last
restriction was removed.[4] Despite changes in legislation, questions
have remained about the appropriate roles for women, the ability of
women to do various jobs, and the equitable participation of
women in the labour force and the military.

From the mid-1970s into the early 1980s, social and behavioural
scientists began to systematically address issues relating to the
impact of women on previously all-male military units. Such
research informed both policy decisions to expand women's
support roles and to undertake research in the area of combat-related employment for women.

For example, in Canada, the Servicewomen in Non-Traditional
Environments and Roles (SWINTER) trials, underpinned by
research and completed in 1985, indicated that the expansion of
women's roles to include isolated and near combat (i.e., combat
support and combat service support), was indeed feasible and, with
some organizational changes, would not impede operational
effectiveness.[5] Further, an analysis of public opinion polls
conducted between 1978 and 1982 concluded that, while overall
Canadian support for women in combat roles was "cautious", it was
increasing over the time of the trials.[6] However, subsequent to the
1989 Tribunal decision, research on women's integration into the
combat arms identified numerous organizational policies and

processes that were still creating substantial barriers to their effective participation.[7] A recent analysis of Canada's experience states that "the degree to which mixed gender integration has occurred in the CF has been...significantly over-stated for the combat arms", and further notes that "once a woman enrolls in the combat arms, the barriers become primarily cultural and social".[8]

Canada is one of an increasing number of nations that actually employ women in the combat arms,[9] since many NATO and other allied nations have removed limitations on the role of women in their militaries. However, at time of writing, combat exclusions remain in place in Australia, France, Turkey, the U.K., and the U.S.[10] While New Zealand currently has a combat exclusion for non-commissioned members, it is implementing a multi-phased integration program with a goal of integration into all roles by 2005.[11] Also, there are a number of cases where general combat exclusions do not exist but where women are excluded from specialized "elite" units. Ireland, for example, does not permit women to serve in the anti-terrorist Army Ranger Wing.[12] To date, women have not served in so-called "assaulter" roles in Canada's elite anti-terrorist unit, Joint Task Force (JTF) 2. Although they are not *formally excluded* from such roles, the physical standards have been set so high that very few women can be expected to meet them or, if they do, to survive the subsequent training process which functions to further "weed out" candidates. The question here is whether the standards applied reflect the *actual* requirement. Greece, the Netherlands, Portugal, and Turkey have exclusions from submarine or other naval service. [13]

Overall, then, various factors can affect the participation rates of women and men in the military, including government-mandated roles and internal values and norms. However, we question the seeming over-emphasis on a warrior ethos that is focused predominantly on combat operations and war-fighting, to the exclusion of other military operations and roles (e.g., peace-support, humanitarian and domestic support) in a military organization in post-modern society. The implications of a primary focus on the warrior framework and women's participation in the military are discussed below.[14]

THE WARRIOR FRAMEWORK UNDER FIRE: CHALLENGING THE TRADITIONAL DEBATE

Much of the commentary on women in the military up to the present time—and most particularly in relation to their ability to adapt to and perform combat roles—has been strongly influenced by socio-cultural perspectives flowing from an exclusively male-oriented warrior framework or at least the assumptions underlying it. Moreover, until recently, much of the social and behavioural science-based evidence has been downplayed or ignored in favour of anecdotal evidence, personal opinion and/or uninformed conjecture. However, fundamental questions have been raised regarding expansion of women's roles, which call for responses based on the evidence available today. Stated quite succinctly in a United States Heritage Foundation article, below are five such questions that permit us to address issues revolving around the physical and mental suitability of women for combat operational roles, the impact of women on group cohesion and effectiveness, and public and personal attitudes toward women in combat. These are:

1. Are women physically suited to the rigors of ground combat?

2. What are the potential consequences of women and men operating in intimate proximity away from home for extended periods of time?

3. What has been the experience of nations that have men and women in mixed combat units?

4. How do women serving in the Armed Forces feel about being assigned to combat units?

5. How will bearing and raising children affect a woman's readiness to deploy on short notice, as is frequently required of military units?[15]

These questions are taken up in turn under the appropriate headings in the paragraphs that follow.

WOMEN'S PHYSICAL SUITABILITY FOR GROUND COMBAT

One of the most important requirements for combat duty is physical fitness, of which aerobic conditioning, strength and endurance form the major part. Perhaps more than any other issue, this has been used most frequently to argue for the exclusion of women from combat. Recent studies, however, cast new light on this matter, and we begin with reference to an example from outside the military.

The New York Fire Department has sought to increase recruitment of women without lowering standards. Physical requirements for both males and females are exceptionally high and have remained unchanged over recent years, translating into much lower rates of success on the part of female applicants. In 2001, only 3 percent of women (11 of 354) who had passed a preliminary written test were successful in an exercise designed to replicate field tasks of serving firefighters. While the comparable success rate for males was 57 percent, the fact remains that some women were able to surmount physical obstacles and become qualified firefighters. More importantly, in terms of future potential, the New York Fire Commissioner has argued that through better recruitment and preparation, more women could meet these strenuous physical requirements.[16]

The US Army Research Institute of Environmental Medicine has gathered evidence pre-dating and consistent with the Fire Commissioner's contention. In a 1995 study involving 41 women volunteers, only 25 percent could perform duties traditionally carried out by men in the military. However, after 24 weeks of training, this proportion rose to 75 percent.[17] Around the same time a United Kingdom (UK) Ministry of Defence concluded that "by using new methods of physical training, women can be built up to the same levels of physical fitness as men of the same size and build."[18] Moreover, the U.S. and other militaries, recognize differential physical aptitude by age but not by gender. The Army Physical Fitness Test (APFT) has varying levels of fitness for those aged 52-56, 57-61 and over 61. "The thought behind this is that a man 62 years of age cannot run a mile in the same time as a man of 19 can."[19] We may wonder, therefore, why some of the same kind of logic cannot be applied to physical differences between men and women.

Some have argued that government (Title IX) regulations in the U.S., requiring schools to provide women with more opportunities for physical exercise, have helped to narrow the strength and endurance gap between the sexes. As an example of this, the male record time for one-mile races fell from 4.12 minutes in 1915 to 3.43 in 1999, a 16.8 percent decline compared to a 32.7 percent drop for women, over roughly the same period, from 6.13 minutes to 4.12 in 1996.[20] The implication here with regard to the physical fitness of women for combat is that with proper training female performance can be enhanced.

A study after the 2000 Summer Olympics showed that most women had greater endurance than most men. In one test, which required participants to hold their arms in a rigid position out from the body, women outlasted men over 75 percent of the time.[21] Further evidence of greater female endurance comes from Witwatersrand

and University of Cape Town studies that found women ran faster than men at longer distances. At the 6.2-, 13.1-, and 26.2-mile distances, most men ran faster than most women. Beyond this distance, however, the situation was reversed, with women outpacing men in races as long as 56 miles.[22] Women can, therefore, match and even exceed, their male counterparts in physical conditioning. All too often, however, the physical ability criteria for inclusion in combat units appear to be both arbitrary and discriminatory to females emphasizing male areas of physical competence.

In 2002, the UK Ministry of Defence conducted one of the most influential studies in recent years on the comparative physical abilities of women and men. On the basis of this work, the U.K. opted not to employ women in combat roles. The review of over 100 studies showed that women had, on average, less upper- and lower-body strength than men, and that fewer than one percent of women could match the average man's strength. Furthermore, women were less aerobically fit and less able to carry out repetitive lifting and carrying tasks. Once more, however, training was shown to dramatically improve women's performance, in that "Women and men exhibit similar relative gains in strength to resistance training programmes … and in some studies, women show a slightly greater gain than men."[23] Furthermore, the same report indicated that aerobic fitness training yielded a greater response among women than men and reduced the aerobic fitness gap between the sexes. As the report points out, this increase may be due to "an initially lower state of training among females on entry to the army"[24] reinforcing arguments made earlier in connection with the United States and the impact of physical education requirements in schools.

CF research has determined that achievement of the same physical standards will not necessarily result in equal performance in an operational environment. For example, all members of the CF must be able to successfully complete five common military tasks: the stretcher carry, sea evacuation, low/high crawl, entrenchment dig, and sandbag carry. The CF has adopted the CF EXPRES test, which accurately predicts a soldier's ability to successfully perform the five basic tasks. Although the test standards are different for women and men, "it has been scientifically determined that a woman who achieves the standard for women on the EXPRES test is as capable of successfully performing the five common tasks as a man who meets the EXPRES test standard." [25]

In 1978, the Canadian Human Rights Commission established a four-step task-related method for the development of physical fitness standards:

1. identify tasks based on operational requirements;

2. identify the physical capability required to complete the tasks;

3. develop appropriate tests which predict the capability to complete the tasks; and

4. set minimum standards based on the tests. [26]

Most occupations and roles in the military are not based on *bona fide* standards established to perform the job. It follows that, in some instances not tied to *bona fide* occupational standards, the lower physical performance of women may simply be irrelevant.

WOMEN AND MEN IN INTIMATE PROXIMITY FOR EXTENDED PERIODS

Most Western societies have integrated workforces where men and women work alongside each other. However, this has not always been the case and is still not common practice in many developing nations. Furthermore, in a military setting, it is argued, close-quarter, mixed-gender operations erode group cohesion and cause stress within combat units. In Canada, for example, one of the objectives of the 1979-1985 trials of Servicewomen in Non-Traditional Environments and Roles (SWINTER) was to determine the impact of women on the operational effectiveness of previously all male units, including impact on 'esprit de corps' .[27] Concern in reference to the impact of women on group cohesion and the link to operational effectiveness was also raised in Canada in the Report of the Charter Task Force on Gender Integration and Sexual Orientation in 1985.[28]

As to group cohesion and effectiveness, important research in the U.S. and elsewhere points to the fact that mixed-gender units do not experience the serious difficulties, as some have proposed. The U.S. Coast Guard has integrated men and women into all aspects of work. As Field and Nagl report, this "is the only service which has no disparities between male and female perceptions of female effectiveness."[29] The same article reported that a 1988 study showed that horizontal cohesion among a group of junior male enlisted soldiers was correlated negatively with the percentage of women in the workplace. A study done seven years later, however, found no relationship between unit cohesion and the presence of women in a work group.

A major study, undertaken by the RAND Corporation in 1997, examined the relationship between various levels of cohesion and females in a group and effects of gender integration on readiness and morale. Divisions caused by gender were seen as minimal in groups with high cohesion, while groups reporting conflict attributed the lack of cohesion primarily to rank and work group divisions; gender played a secondary role.[30] Morale was seen to be affected mainly by leadership, while gender effects were reported to be distinctly minor. [31]

A Ministry of Defence study in Britain concluded that "contrary to the view of traditionalists, the operational performance of groups improves greatly if both sexes are involved."[32] The Ministry conducted an experiment in 2000 to investigate more closely the relationship between various aspects of group cohesion and operational performance and the presence of women in combat units; one all-male and five mixed-gender groups were subjected to a series of demanding tests and routines. Differences in cohesion and military performance were measured and observed but, as the report concluded, "Leadership and teamwork ...were more important in explaining variation between sections than gender mix."[33]

EXPERIENCE OF NATIONS WITH MIXED MEN AND WOMEN IN COMBAT UNITS

Historically, some countries (e.g., Russia; Israel) have employed women in combat units in times of war, and then either disbanded such units shortly after the conflict or reverted to using women in more traditional roles. This has been taken by some as an indicator of the failure of women in these roles. However, such decisions may be guided more by political, cultural or religious influences than by tactical or organizational considerations.

In recent years, court decisions and public pressure have led to militaries opening more jobs to women. Since a human rights case was decided against the Bundeswehr, Germany now permits women in combat units, thus joining Canada, Denmark, Norway, Spain, and Sweden in opening up all military positions to women. Some have argued that these countries do not represent good examples of possible dangers of mixed-gender combat units because they have not played leading roles in recent years in waging war. As a UK Ministry of Defence report put it in 2002, "Those nations that optimize their forces for high-intensity warfare, who see war fighting rather than operations other than war (OOTW) or peacekeeping as their purpose, appear most cautious about deploying women in combat units."[34] This assumes, of course, that countries that may participate more frequently in peace support and humanitarian operations never go to war and that their militaries do not view themselves as combat-capable forces. This is certainly not the case for many of the countries that allow women in combat roles. Indeed, it can be argued that Canada, for example, has been to war almost as often as the United Kingdom, at least since 1914. Also, peace support operations undertaken since the end of the Cold War often have had combat-related requirements that closely resembled war-fighting.

The two countries that have been most often cited as positive examples of the impact of mixed-gender combat units are Israel and the former U.S.S.R. Neither country currently permits women in combat although over one million Russian women fought during the Second World War in close combat, in tanks, and in planes. As a U.K. report acknowledged, "There is no question that they were effective."[35]

During the Israeli War of Independence, women fought in frontline positions, but this has not been the case since 1948. While various reasons have been given for this withdrawal, including the unacceptability of women being killed in battle, it has been accepted that, "Arab soldiers fought more determinedly against women rather than risk disgrace by surrendering to them."[36] Furthermore, recent controversy over the same issue in Israel has revealed strong religious objections to the integration of women in all positions. A leading Rabbi pointed to the fact that for religious soldiers the maintenance of Jewish law (Halacha) was impossible where men and women had to share close quarters.[37] Although this is now widely recognized as a cultural issue, some have erroneously argued, and continue to maintain, that this is an example of the negative impact of women on combat effectiveness.

Many countries have now had at least some experience of mixed-gender military units, with little evidence of negative impacts on effectiveness, cohesion, or readiness. Military fears about mistreatment of female prisoners have been realized, with at least two instances of abuse in the Gulf War. At least one of these captives has asserted that while she had suffered abuse, she "had been treated no differently from any of the men."[38]

WOMEN'S VIEWS ABOUT BEING ASSIGNED TO COMBAT UNITS

The issue here is whether or not women are interested in being employed in combat units and roles, the degree to which such is the case and the basis for their views one way or the other.

In a survey of 112 female cadets at West Point in the 1990s, Field and Nagl found that only 30 percent would join a combat arms branch if these were opened up to women. Only a small proportion of this group (13 percent) would have opted for infantry positions rather than other branches, such as armour and field artillery, which the researchers noted are "less associated with difficult field conditions, physically arduous tasks and hand-to-hand fighting".[39] Only 12 percent of the sample with no desire to enter combat units cited a lack of faith in their physical capabilities as motivating their decision; most (65 percent) were just not interested in combat arms.[40] While only 30 percent of women in this study expressed interest in the combat arms, interest among men is often similar. A 1999 CF study measured interest in volunteering for submarine service before such service was open to women;[41] in this case, the difference in interest expressed by women and men who had no experience in submarines was much less pronounced than the differences between men with and without submarine experience.[42] Increased exposure for women to combat positions will no doubt have the same impact as that of making such positions more appealing and interesting.

The 2002 UK Ministry of Defence study indicated that more than half of the women surveyed supported the involvement of women in combat units as opposed to only half the men.[43]

CHILDBEARING, CHILDREARING AND WOMEN'S READINESS TO DEPLOY ON SHORT NOTICE

Group cohesion is seen as an essential element of combat units. Building group cohesion takes time. Members of the unit must share common experiences and build confidence in each other. The fact that women can become pregnant and require time off to give birth and nurse children has been argued as having a potentially negative impact on such cohesion-building efforts. However, among other things, this argument ignores the fact that extended absences from units can be caused by many reasons, pregnancy being one of the least important.

Within the United States Army, almost 14 percent of personnel are non-deployable and only 0.79 percent of women are pregnant at any given time. While this rate has been as high as 10 percent in some units, it is still somewhat below the average US non-deployable level.[44] In other words, pregnancy as a cause for lack of deployability is of minor significance compared to other, non gender-specific causes, and so presents less of a problem regarding replacement than might be supposed.

In some instances, fairly high rates of pregnancy have been recorded among mixed-gender units, leading some to argue against the inclusion of women in the forces. In August 1996, 70 American military personnel – 4.6 percent of the women stationed in Bosnia – were removed to Germany when they became pregnant. During the Gulf War, the USS Arcadia was dubbed the "Love Boat" after losing 36 of its 360 women sailors to pregnancy.[46] Indeed, some would contend that some women become pregnant to avoid going into combat. Regardless of the cause, young women of childbearing age will become pregnant in any occupation but, given the critical nature of some military roles, it has been suggested that an easy answer is to apply a birth-control requirement to women wishing to serve in combat units if it appeared that disruptions might occur.[47] While this may be a solution, it has also been noted that pregnancy is simply one of many social issues and medical conditions that *may interfere with the deployment or repatriation of a soldier*. It has not been established that rates of pregnancy in mixed-gender operational environments are greater than the rate of pregnancy witnessed among the female population as a whole. Other industries and employers have developed suitable human resources policies to manage absences from positions by employees for this and a host of other reasons. There would appear to be no logical reason why militaries could not make the same accommodations for women in combat that are already made for those not in combat units.

In a 1997 study of propensity to join the CF, women were twice as likely as men to cite family or children as their most important reason for having no interest in joining the military.[48] However, for most parts, those women who do choose to join are likely to have considered family-related issues and are also making a choice similar to that of men, relative to their current or future family obligations. Although women in general still have disproportionate responsibility for raising children, men increasingly share this role; therefore, except in one-parent situations, the burden of family should be looked upon as a joint responsibility. Finally, similar to other large-scale employers, the military has recognized that morale, motivation and retention of women and men depend on policies that provide greater ability to balance the demands of family and service to the organization. Overall, such policies form part of the overall human resource support structure of most Western-style, contemporary militaries—the CF included.

THE WARRIOR FRAMEWORK

Research over the past two decades has identified numerous barriers to the integration of women into various military roles. We suggest that warrior attributes expressed through such terms as "warrior ethos", "warrior culture", and "warrior spirit" increasingly dominate the development of military policy and doctrine. In addition, we propose that this shift is gaining legitimacy within military organizations at a time when research has started to identify skills and attributes *other than traditional warrior attributes* as more and more significant for the future. While the research of the 1980s and 1990s measured the participation and integration of women in the military by means of various social science approaches and methodologies, notions of warrior ethos, warrior spirit, and warrior attributes have not been tested within an objective framework that considers both operational effectiveness and gender equality.

Observations as early as 1992 describe a shift in the focus of the debates surrounding women's rights to military service, from the historical focus on military necessity to a focus on values.[49] The warrior framework is similar to, if not the same as, what Karen Dunivin identified in 1994 as the combat masculine war-fighting (CMW) model, asserting that such a model focuses on war fighting or combat as the central focus of military activity.[50] Similarly, Judith Youngman's analysis of the shift in the US from the citizen soldier to the warrior ethic and culture notes that "understanding the *warrior* and the *warrior culture* is essential for understanding the military at the end of the twentieth century."[51] Warrior ethos and the warrior ethic have been defined in various ways to convey the central elements and values of the culture, including moral and ethical courage, tactical skills, emotional and physical stamina, loyalty to comrades, and determination to accomplish the mission.[52] While many would argue that the warrior framework is uniquely applied to the combat arms,[53] there is an increasing emphasis on "warrior-like" characteristics as essential to all military roles. As noted by Thomas St. Denis, "No one serving today in the armies of Canada or the United States is any longer just a soldier. Increasingly, he or she is a 'warrior', a term overloaded with philosophical and behavioural connotations."[54] In a recent example, a US report on training and leader development states: "The warrior ethos is a part of the foundation of Army Culture, along with the service ethic, Army values, and lifelong learning. It includes every soldier in the profession, excluding none."[55]

Proponents of the warrior ethos claim that there is not a shared meaning of the warrior ethos or warrior ethic; however, Youngman argues that historically, the warrior is understood to be male and assumed to share such characteristics as superior physical and moral attributes, aggressive nature, proclivity to violence, rite of passage marked by physical prowess, "will to kill", masculinity, and embodiment of virtue. She asserts, "the warrior and warrior culture reflect more than mere changes in words used to describe the ideal American soldier. The emergence of the "new" warrior in American military culture and the increasing glorification of the warrior in popular culture reflect a fundamental redefinition of the ideal American soldier."[56] Youngman identifies several values and gender-based arguments put forward within a warrior framework opposed to the inclusion of women in the combat arms.[57] In response, she notes that those who oppose the pro-male, pro-warrior arguments have successfully countered each of the arguments supporting the warrior framework. For example, in response to the need for male bonding, she notes that cross-gender bonding did occur in the Gulf War and continues among deployed troops.[58] Youngman concludes that "the treatment of women in the warrior culture, therefore, appears to be based on assumptions unrelated to women's abilities and aptitude to perform combat jobs".[59]

As organizations of all kinds come to rely increasingly on performance-measurement frameworks, proponents of the warrior perspective remain dependent upon arguments that are rooted in traditional notions of gender differences, rather than on results of objective examination. The discussion presented earlier looked at a similar set of questions and concerns put forward by a "right wing" think tank, a framework that is characteristic of the concerns presented within warrior frameworks. Each of the issues was in turn addressed, albeit in a cursory manner, by concepts, research, and experience that suggest a more reliable platform upon which to base decisions relating to current and future participation of women in the military. These are not new issues; rather, they are concerns that have been dismissed as organizations, including the military, have moved ahead with efforts to integrate women. However, we have witnessed recent decisions regarding women's participation, such as the 2002 UK Ministry of Defence decision to continue to exclude women from participation in close combat roles,[60] that are not based on research and experience. Instead, decisions reflect what proponents of a male-centric warrior culture believe to be true in spite of the available research. The implications of a framework based on anything other than research and experience for the service of women in the military today and in the future are discussed below.

RECONFIGURING THE DEBATE: SOLDIERS OF THE FUTURE

The traditional arguments of women's physical and mental suitability for warfare appear to have been effectively countered by growing evidence showing that many women would be able to participate at a level comparable to men if given the proper training, orientation and leadership. Nor have the assertions of a negative impact of women on group cohesion and effectiveness been supported by empirical evidence, as the examples above have shown. More than this, even those governments that have been most ardent in their opposition to female involvement in combat have not exempted women from "near-combat" roles. As a recent article in an American military newspaper indicated, female soldiers have been employed in combat areas in Afghanistan to help in the search for weapons and Al-Qaeda operatives, because the Muslim population would not tolerate frisking and body searches of females by males.[61]

Most recently, debate has shifted somewhat, and new arguments have sprung up about the issue of women in combat, centred on human rights and new technology. A 2001 article by Anna Simons, claiming that allowing US women in combat was "still a bad idea", summarizes the new configuration of questions well: "New post-Cold War missions require finesse, not brawn....Twenty-first century technologies are gender-neutral."[62] The definition of warfare and the role of the military have changed dramatically in the wake of the fall of the communist regimes of Eastern Europe. Alongside the new roles of peace building and peacekeeping, militaries have increasingly faced a wider diversity of conflict situations, ranging from conventional war to urban terrorism and guerilla skirmishes.

The weaponry and skill sets needed to perform the duties of the modern military have changed, suggesting the need to consider a range of psychological, physical and cognitive competencies that go beyond absolute brute strength and "brawn". This does not mean that physical fitness, physical conditioning and training are not important, but does argue that *brute strength and brawn* is not a *bona fide* occupational requirement. For example, in a 1997 survey of 3,505 Swedish peacekeepers rotating through Bosnia in the early 1990s resulted in an identification of the qualities of the "ideal" UN soldier:

> *Not a Rambo*, flexible, humble, adaptable, able to resist frustration, tolerant, able to show feelings, group-orientated, patient, staying power, manage stress, self-

confidence, tough, obstinate, able to listen, tolerates provocation, impartial, and diplomatic. The study further highlighted the following statement: "In the first place, be a good human being, not just a good soldier."[63]

A 1999 conference in Uppsala, Sweden, explored "Mainstreaming Gender in Multilateral Peacekeeping Operations". Sponsored by the United Nations, this conference looked at the impact of higher proportions of women in peacekeeping units. Among other conclusions: the presence of women in conflict areas tends to defuse confrontation and violence to a much greater extent than the presence of armed men.[64] In Somalia, the US Army found that all-male combat units quickly developed hostile attitudes to the local population and were more prone to use force than were support units. These latter contained women and were more likely to "exhibit a strong inclination to understand the problems facing the host society".[65]

As the previously cited example of the female American soldiers in Afghanistan also demonstrates, militaries now face many more situations where cultural or other constraints make it necessary to include women in front-line duties. The continued use of rape as a weapon of war, as was the case in Bosnia where 50,000 civilians were sexually assaulted, may be a further argument for the inclusion of women in combat units: the presence of women may lead to different behaviour on the part of men in military units. Furthermore, as one British recruitment military advertisement has suggested, these situations may require women to help deal with the aftermath of such atrocities.[66]

Increased use of technology, rather than brawn, is becoming a hallmark of modern warfare. The days of mass infantry ground attacks are less prevalent, at least for most militaries in developed nations. Actions by the U.S. and the U.K. in the Falklands, the Persian Gulf,

and Afghanistan have required fewer ground troops and more precision bombing. Guided, heat-sensitive missiles operated from a
distance have created an increasing demand for skilled operators
rather than hardened troops. In a study of child soldiers conducted
for the United Nations, Graça Machel observed that "modern
weapons technology makes it easy to use child soldiers: modern
automatic weapons are so light and so easily taken apart and put
together again that they can be put in the hands of children."[67]
There is abundant evidence that the requirements of soldiering are
changing, thus underlining the importance of evolving standards
based on *bona fide* requirements to achieve the mission. As noted as
far back as 1969, in a US Court of Appeals Decision, "labeling a job
'strenuous' simply does not meet the burden of proof that the job is
within the bona fide occupational qualification exception."[68] While
physical strength and stamina do continue to play a role in soldier
effectiveness, the question remains as to whether the same physical
standards are required to achieve the missions of modern militaries.

CONCLUSION

The above discussion has focused on some of the key issues of
concern over the role of women in the military and highlights the
implications for their role in the future. It is clear that many, if not
most, of the arguments and decisions that limit the participation of
women in a full range of military roles and environments are not
based upon what we have learned through experience and research.
While some of the developing trends are clear, many questions
remain largely unanswered. What is the future role of the military
within the broader security environment? To what extent will
technology influence the nature of war? To what extent will
military services and operations be provided by privatized industry,
both in support roles and operational activities by "mercenary"
forces? How will all of these things affect military ethos, the
warrior framework, and the role of women?

For some time, analysts have argued that socio-cultural issues, from the perspective of a warrior framework, represent significant barriers to the integration of women into the military and, in particular, into current and recent all-male roles. We would add that warrior frameworks, which have traditionally been associated with the combat arms and direct combat-related military service, are increasingly applied to a broad range of military environments and roles. From a historical perspective, there has been significant success with the integration of women into the combat arms. However, from a contemporary perspective, progress is surprisingly slow when considered in comparison with the progress of women into previously all-male domains in the civilian labour force as a whole.

Finally, we suggest that the notion of "every soldier as a warrior" represents a "warrior-creep" that is not based on *bona fide* requirements to get the job done, regardless of the sex of the individual. "Warrior-creep" represents a significant barrier to the integration of women, as well as increasing proportions of men, as values and lifestyles in our democratic societies evolve. What remains unclear is the extent to which these arguments are about the power, politics, and economy that influence the status of women more broadly, and the extent to which these same arguments will affect the operational effectiveness of the military.

NOTES

1   For historical data on women's participation in the Canadian labour force and the federal public service in Canada, see Minister of Supply and Services Canada, *Beneath the Veneer: The Report of the Task Force on Barriers to Women in the Public Service* (Ottawa: Canadian Government Publishing Centre, 1990).

2   See, for example, N. J. Holden and L. M. Tanner, *An Examination of Current Gender Integration Policies and Practices in TTCP Countries* (Ottawa: Director Strategic Human Resource Coordination, Personnel Operational Research Team & Director Military Gender Integration and Employment Equity, ORD Report R2001/01), for a historical overview of women's participation in the militaries of The Technical Cooperation Panel.

3   Canadian Human Rights Commission, Tribunal Decision 3/89 *BETWEEN: ISABELLE GAUTHIER, JOSEPH G. HOULDEN, MARIE-CLAUDE GAUTHIER, GEORGINA ANN*

BROWN Complainants and CANADIAN ARMED FORCES Respondent (Decision rendered on February 20, 1989).

4   National Defence, *Mixed Gender Crewing of Victoria Class Submarines* (Ottawa: NDHQ MARGEN 016/01 CMS 021/01, 2001).

5   R. E. Park, *Overview of the Social/Behavioural Science Evaluation of the 1979-1985 Canadian Forces Trial Employment of Servicewomen in Non-Traditional Environments and Roles*, Research Report 86-2 (Willowdale, ON: Canadian Forces Personnel Applied Research Unit, 1986).

6   R. E. Park, *Public Opinion and the Placement of Canadian Forces' Servicewomen in Combat*, Paper presented at the 20th International Applied Military Psychology Symposium, Brussels, 1984.

7   K. D. Davis, *Chief Land Staff Gender Integration Study: The Experience of Women Who have Served in the Combat Arms*, Sponsor Research Report 98-1 (Ottawa: Personnel Research Team National Defence, 1998).

8   Franklin C. Pinch, Selected Issues and Constraints on Full Gender Integration in Elite Ground Combat Units in Canada (Kingston, ON: FCP Human Resources Consulting, 2002).

9   The Czech Republic, Denmark, Hungary, Netherlands, Norway, Austria and Ireland have women serving in combat arms occupations. See Committee on Women in the NATO Forces, *Teambuilding Towards New Challenges*, Member nation and Partnership for Peace reports to the Annual Meeting of the Committee of Women in NATO Forces, Brussels, 2002.

10   Committee on Women in the NATO Forces, *Teambuilding Towards New Challenges*.

11   Holden and Tanner, *An Examination of Current Gender Integration Policies and Practices in TTCP Countries*.

12   Committee on Women in the NATO Forces, *Teambuilding Towards New Challenges*.

13   Ibid.

14   For example, see K. D. Davis, *The Future of Women in the Canadian Forces: Defining the Strategic Human Resource Challenge*, DSHRC Research Note 10/01 (Ottawa: Director of Strategic Human Resources Coordination, National Defence, 2001).

15   John Luddy, "Congress Should Hold Hearings Before Allowing Women in Combat," *Heritage Foundation Backgrounder* #230. (Washington: The Heritage Foundation, 1994).

16   Kim Field and John Nagl, "Combat Roles for Women: A Modest Proposal," *Parameters* (Summer 2001): 6.

17   B. Wilson, "Women in Combat: Why not?" http://userpages.aug.com/captbarb/combat.html

18   Ibid.: 1.

19   L. Casey, "Women in Combat": 3. http://www.militarywoman.org/academic.htm

20   Field and Nagl, "Combat Roles for Women": 8.

21   C. Prandzik, "Runners Life: Want better endurance, be female study suggests," *Army Times* (13 May 2002): 1.

22   Ibid.: 2.

23   Ministry of Defence, "Women in the Armed Forces". (London: Ministry of Defence, 2002): B-4.

24   Ibid.

25   The Army Lessons Learned Centre, "Lessons Learned – Leadership in a Mixed Gender Environment" Despatches (Kingston, ON: National Defence, 1998): 21.

26   Wayne S. Lee, "Setting the Record Straight: Land Force Command Physical Fitness Standards and Programs," *Defence* 2000 News (September 1999).

27   National Defence, Telcon Directorate of Military Gender Integration and Employment Equity 3-7 (Ottawa, 25 September 2002).

28   Field and Nagl, "Combat Roles for Women": 82.

29   Ibid.

30   M. C. Harrell and L. M. Miller, *New Opportunities for Military Women: Effects Upon Readiness, Cohesion, and Morale* (Santa Monica, CA and Washington, D.C.: National Defense Research Institute RAND, 1997).

31   Harrell and Miller, *New Opportunities for Military Women*

32   Wilson, "Women in Combat": 1.

33   Ministry of Defence, "Women in the Armed Forces" (London: MoD, 2002): 15.

34   Ibid., 13.

35   Ibid., 12.

36   Ibid.

37   *Jerusalem Post*, "Gender Skirmishes in the IDF," 6 August 2001: 6.

38   J. Hoffman, "Men and Children First," *American Spectator*, September 1992: 43.

39   Field and Nagl, "Combat Roles for Women": 6.

40   Ibid., 7.

41   J. E. Adams-Roy. Service in Canadian Forces Submarines: Exploring the Attitudes of Naval Personnel towards Volunteer Service and Mixed Gender Crews, Sponsor Research Report 99-8 (Ottawa: Director Human Resources Research and Evaluation Sponsor, 1999).

42   Adams-Roy, *Service in Canadian Forces Submarines*; 30.7 percent of men and 26.6 percent of women with no submarine experience indicated that they were either a "Possible Volunteer" or had a "Definite Interest in Volunteering", while 50 percent of men who were submarine-qualified (previous or current submarine service) indicated that they were interested in returning to submarine service. All men and women surveyed were currently serving in hard sea occupations.

43   Ministry of Defence, "Women in the Armed Forces": 13.

44   Field and Nagl, "Combat Roles for Women": 7.

45   Casey, "Women in Combat".

46   B. Gerber, "Women in the Military and Combat" (1998), http://www.military-woman.org/academic.htm

47   Field and Nagl, "Combat Roles for Women": 7.

48   Davis, The Future of Women in the Canadian Forces, 14.

49   Mady Weschler Segal and Amanda Faith Hansen, "Value Rationales in Policy Debates on Women in the Military," *Social Science Quarterly* 73, 2 (June 1992).

50   Pinch, Selected Issues and Constraints.

51   Judith Youngman, "The Warrior Ethic," in *Women in Uniform: Perceptions and Pathways*, Kathryn Spurling, and Elizabeth Greenlaugh, eds. (Canberra: School of History, Australian Defence Force Academy, 2000), 36.

52   Centre for Strategic and International Studies, Project on *Military Culture for the 21st Century*, Working Paper (20 October 1998), cited in Youngman, "The Warrior Ethic".

53   See, for example, Charles Moskos, "From Citizen's Army to Social Laboratory," *Wilson Quarterly* 17, 1 (Winter 1993): 84; Don M. Snider, "An Uninformed Debate in Military Culture," Orbis 43, 1 (Winter 1999): 11-26, cited in Youngman, "The Warrior Ethic".

54   Thomas St. Denis, "The Dangerous Appeal of the Warrior," *Canadian Military Journal* 2, 2 (Summer 2001):

55   Ibid., 31.

56   Youngman, "The Warrior Ethic": 49.

57   Ibid., 43.

58   Ibid., 44.

59   Ibid., 45.

60   Ministry of Defence, "Women in the Armed Forces".

61   European Stars and Stripes, 16 September 2002.

62   Anna Simons, "Women in Combat Units: It's still a bad idea," *Parameters* (Summer 2001): 89.

63   Eva Johansson, In a Blue Beret: Four Swedish UN battalions in Bosnia, LI, 'R' Series. R:1

64   G.R. DeGroot, "Women as Peacekeepers," *Toronto Star*, 25 July 1999.

65   See L. Miller and Charles C. Moskos, "Humanitarians or Warriors?: Race, Gender, and Combat Status in Operation Restore Hope," *Armed Forces and Society* Vol. 21 (4) (Summer 1995): 615-637.

66   DeGroot, "Women as Peacekeepers".

67   Michael Ignatieff, The Warrior's Honour: Ethnic War and the Modern Conscience (Toronto: Penguin Books, 1999), 127.

68   Cited in Joyce Hogan and Ann M. Quigley, "Physical Standards for Employment and the Courts," *American Psychologist* 41, 11 (1986): 1196.

WOMEN IN THE FRENCH FORCES:
INTEGRATION VERSUS CONFLICT[1]

KATIA SORIN

INTRODUCTION

Until the recent reorganization of the French armed forces,[2] few studies were available on the role of women in those organizations.[3] In response to requests for proposals issued by the Armed Forces via *le Centre d'études en sciences sociales*,[4] a number of large-scale studies have been undertaken, both within the military[5] and by civilian researchers. In the midst of a growing need for "manpower", France's military leaders began to give more recognition to the existence of women: in fact, the availability of many highly qualified women who offered good value for the cost involved. This interest in women was a pragmatic response to a perceived organizational requirement. The research thrust was, first, to identify this "pool" of women; second, to determine their motivations; and, third, to analyze the process of integrating women: all in order to make the decisions necessary for it to be accomplished under more favourable conditions than existed previously. This chapter is about some of the most problematic issues with gender integration in the French military, mainly as seen through the eyes of the women themselves.

RESEARCH CONTEXT

In France, as elsewhere, the field of war and military matters has, until recently, been regarded as an exclusively male preserve. Men alone have had the legitimate right to engage in combat and, for a long time, military service was regarded as the most important phase in a young man's progression to manhood. The latter included an emphasis on masculinity, defined by such qualities as courage, tolerance of pain, sense of sacrifice, physical strength, solidarity, and even patriotism – qualities in contrast to those attributed by society to women. The aim was thus to distance military men as far as possible from the image of femininity, the object at once of all desires and all fears. The inclusion of women thus overturned this order of things, to the extent that it has called into question a definition of the military institution based on a markedly hierarchical role distinction between the sexes.

Moreover, this institutional "discontinuity" merely exacerbates an environment in which the traditional bearings are being lost in a military that is in a state of constant flux – a situation that men in the armed forces have difficulty accepting and adjusting to. Warfare has changed, with man-to-man combat no longer the norm; most of today's soldiers have never taken part in intense armed conflict. Since one of the new features of military missions and operations is their ambiguity – in that they combine humanitarian, political/diplomatic, social reconstruction, and military dimensions – military personnel are asking many questions about their role, their usefulness, and hence the meaning of their commitment. Such questions have become louder since the start of the reforms of France's defence establishment: the restructuring of the forces with the end of conscription; the disbanding of units; the operational reorganization of the forces; the overall reduction in strength, together with a rapid increase in the number of non-commissioned members; and the creation of new types of purely contractual engagements. In these changing and uncertain circumstances, the strong reaction of men to the presence of increasing numbers of women is understandable: apart from the other upheavals, it is their own masculinity, their own self-image – in short, their own *raison d'être* as soldiers – that is crumbling.

RESEARCH QUESTIONS

From the above considerations derives the perception that women's entry into non-traditional roles in the French military – actually the women themselves – will probably compromise the established order. It leads us to the proposition that military women are stigmatized, in Erving Goffman's sense,[6] simply because they do not have those socially legitimate qualities that define soldiers. Women merely infringe on the social norms within which the institution of the armed forces – and, to some extent, the larger society – operates. Woman and Soldier together constitute a concept that is not socially "natural". The objective of the study on which this chapter is based was to understand the responses provoked by this stigmatization, not only among men, but among the women themselves. For example, how are women reacting? What logical approaches and strategies do they draw upon to find their place within the armed forces and to harmonize their dual status, in terms of femininity and physical and social realities? For what reasons and with what aims? Thus, the study aimed to explore as exhaustively as possible the way in which the women view their place and their integration into the armed forces, both individually and as a gender-defined group.

SAMPLE AND METHODOLOGY

Since the original study was concerned first and foremost with women's perceptions of their experience in the military, the data were collected through semi-directed interviews. A sample of 248 female military personnel[7] was selected, with a view to obtaining a varied range of sociological profiles, based on a number of criteria: the service to which they belonged, rank, occupational classification, unit, age, and marital and family status. The breakdown by these factors is shown on the next page in Table 1.

The study sample is atypical in that there is an over-representation of cadets, officers, sailors, and airwomen and of operational units for the Navy and Army, and an under-representation of administrative occupations. The fact that the sample is unrepresentative of the total population is not inherently problem-

LOCATION	Units - 203; training schools - 45.
RANK	Officers - 46; Non-commissioned officers - 19; Other ranks - 39; Officer cadets - 15; Non-commissioned officer cadets - 30.
SERVICE	Army - 76; Navy - 79; Air Force - 87; Gendarmerie - 5; Health Professional (pharmacist) - 1.
MILITARY OCCUPATIONS REPRESENTED	Administration - 40%; signals - 13%; electronics technician - 12%; mechanic - 10%; air traffic control - 5%; computer technician - 4%; medical/health - 4%; air medical escort; instructor, meteorologist, boatswain, firefighter, pilot, rifleman - commando - 12%.
TYPE OF UNIT	Operational units - 70%; Headquarters - 20%; Schools - 10%.
AGE	19 to 30 years of age - 57%; 31 to 57 - 43%.

SOURCE: KATIA SORIN, FEMMES EN ARMES: UNE PLACE INTROUVABLE ? LE CAS DE LA FÉMINISATION DES ARMÉES FRANÇAISES, DOCTORAL THESIS IN SOCIOLOGY, PARIS 1 PANTHÉON-SORBONNE, 2002, CHAPTER 3.

TABLE 1. PRINCIPAL CHARACTERISTICS OF THE SAMPLE

atic, since the objective was intra-sample diversity, with no intention of generalizing results to the whole population of women in the French Forces. The study focussed on women in traditional male environments and roles, where their presence was hypothesized to be seen as most disruptive and where male resistance was likely to be most intense: in operational units (regiments, frigates, naval air stations), rather than in Headquarters, where they worked as secretaries, for example. Furthermore, this large number of interviews and the diversity of individual profiles allowed for complementary analyses, both qualitative (thematic) and quantitative (statistical), of the interviews. Thus, it was possible to identify fairly detailed comparisons on matters such as those involving motivation or so-called "physical barriers" – a task reported upon after a brief summary of the evolution of women in the French armed forces.

A BACKGROUND SUMMARY

The history of women in the French Forces can be divided into four main periods, the first of which dates back to World War II, when women first enrolled in the forces, under a status that, while unquestionably civilian, made them subject to military regulations. They were recruited under contract for the duration of the war only and in a limited number of areas, such as health, administration, and data processing. At the end of the war, only a minority remained in the forces and were involved a few years later in the war in Indochina.

The second period began in 1951, the year in which a corps of servicewomen was established in peacetime. They were recruited on renewable contracts and received true military status, albeit a status parallel to that of men, i.e., subject to its own rules. Their military training was quite brief: their hierarchy was neither nominally nor organizationally integrated within the male hierarchy, and instead of ranks they had "classes" (for officers) and "categories" (for non-commissioned officers); their career progression was very slow, particularly for officers; uniforms were different; and finally, very few occupational specialities were open to them – the same ones, in fact, as were available during World War II. There was no real change in this situation until the early 1970s.

The third period was characterized by the gradual blending of status. This resulted initially from the Act of July 13, 1972, regarding the general status of military personnel, which draws no distinction between men and women in terms of status structure, promotion, pay, restrictions, etc. For example, women were given access to career status and could hold a military rank. However, the decree of March 23, 1973 – on the specific status of the women's corps in the armed forces, which managed the transition – set significant restrictions. Training was segregated and was adminis- tered from that year on within a joint service women's school, *École interarmées du personnel militaire féminin* (EIPMF). Women had achieved access to careers that were equivalent to, albeit statutorily separate from, those of men, since they had their own corps. This special status was abrogated in 1975-1976. Women officers were incorporated into some male corps, but not into the most prestigious positions, such as the rank structure of combat arms officer (Army), seagoing officer (Navy), and flying officer[8] (Air Force). Their access to occupations was still very limited.

The fourth period began in 1981, with the creation of the commission on the future of women in the armed forces, *la Commission d'étude prospective de la femme militaire*. Its work ended with the submission of a report to the French Minister of Defence, which outlined a number of proposals for improving the circumstances of women in the forces, a high proportion of which were implemented over the next 15 years. The first major decision was the closure of EIPMF in 1983; non-commissioned officers of both sexes would henceforth be trained in the same schools. A number of specialities were opened up to women, although their recruitment was subject to maximum quotas.[9]

The following are the dates of some key events:

- 1983: opening of the Gendarmerie; opening of the École Spéciale Militaire at Saint-Cyr; beginning of the trial period for women in surface ships (until 1987); women now permitted to serve in all Army regiments;

- 1986: opening of recruiting for transport and helicopter pilots under contract only; access to the Navy's non-commissioned officer corps;

- 1992: institutionalization of women at sea; opening of the Naval Academy;

- 1995: opening of the fighter pilot classification in the Air Force (1999 in the Navy);

- 1998: opening of the classification of rifleman-commando in the Army (1999 in the Navy); abolition of recruiting quotas;

- 2000: opening of all combat arms occupations in the Army.

CURRENT SITUATION

Today, only those specialties that require service at sea in submarines and a career as a non-commissioned member in the Gendarmerie Mobile are still closed to women. This does not mean, however, that women have a significant presence in all occupations or that equality in terms of the division of work by gender has been achieved. In October 2000, there were almost 32,000 women in uniform, representing slightly under 10 percent of total career members. As Table 2 indicates, 5 percent of officers, 9 percent of non-commissioned officers (NCOs), 11 percent of other ranks (ORs), and 18 percent of volunteers[10] are women.

	ARMY	AIR FORCE	NAVY	GND[a]	SSA[b]	DGA[c]	OTHER	TOTAL
OFFICERS	4	5	5	1	17	9	5	5
NCOS	11	11	8	5	59	13	8	10
ORS	8	26	7	-	27	-	6	11
VOLUNTEERS	19	35	4	17	51	-	-	18
TOTAL	9	14	8	6	40	10	6	9

NOTE: 4 PERCENT OF ARMY OFFICERS ARE WOMEN.
[a] GENDARMERIE; [b] SERVICE DE SANTÉ DES ARMÉES; [c] DÉLÉGATION GÉNÉRALE DE L'ARMEMENT.

TABLE 2. PERCENTAGE OF WOMEN IN EACH SERVICE CATEGORY,
         OCTOBER 2000[11]

Table 1 also shows that the numerical status of women differs among the services, since the joint services Medical Corps has by far the highest female representation, followed by the Air Force. In the case of the former, this high proportion is due above all to the majority being female nursing NCOs, while female medical officers are in the minority.[12]   In the second case, if the Army and the officer corps are combined, it is apparent that the high percentage of women in the Air Force is due to their greater representation among other ranks, whereas the figures with regard to NCOs and officers are virtually equivalent. Otherwise, officers are proportionately less numerous than are ORs, and in the more senior ranks, women are virtually absent. Furthermore, at current recruiting rates, it is conceivable that there will be little significant improvement in the coming years, since the female population is regarded more as a surplus to maintain high recruiting levels than as a true target population.[13]

Nonetheless, as can be seen from Table 3, the percentage of women who submit their files for an NCO competition is far from negligible, and this is probably the primary reason for the high selection rate they are experiencing. There are some possible explanations: for example, the Navy has established unofficial quotas because of the limited number of warships available to women. The type of diploma held by an applicant is also a factor, particularly for technical occupations, as a higher percentage of women have degrees in the arts and in administration.

	ARMY (1999)	AIR FORCE (1998)	NAVY (1999)	GENDARMERIE (1998)
% of candidates	36	43	39	21
% of recruits	17	25	21	9

TABLE 3. DIRECT RECRUITING OF FEMALE NCOS

Table 4 shows the proportion of females as candidates for the three military academies and as recruits. The conditions of recruiting for officers[14] and the anti-female image of the Army go a long way towards explaining the low number of female candidates for the military academies – together, in the case of the Army and, to a lesser extent, the Navy, with more rigorous selection processes for them. For example, the most difficult stage for young female candidates is the oral one, which is the point at which anonymity is no longer maintained and so the candidate's gender becomes known. This finding has been amply demonstrated in connection with other competitions for the French public service. Furthermore, it is clear that there are more female candidates in other types of direct officer recruiting. In the Army, 40 percent of civilian candidates for the *Corps technique et administratif* (CTA) are female, and there, again, the selection process is far more rigorous, since women represented only one quarter of the recruits in 1998 and one third in 1999. Similarly, women are much more numerous in the "recruiting for officers on contract" category. Thus, a quarter of officers recruited on contract in the Navy in 2000 were women, compared to 14 percent the previous year.

	ARMY (1999)	AIR FORCE (1998)	NAVY (1999)
% of candidates	10	10	14
% of recruits	4	10	11

TABLE 4. RECRUITMENT OF FEMALE OFFICERS FROM THE MILITARY ACADEMIES [15]

DEMOGRAPHIC AND SERVICE PROFILES

The study also compared the profile of service personnel on the basis of gender to determine whether or not the female military population is specific and, if so, in what respect. From the sparse data available, the analysis shows that women in fact constitute a slightly distinct population, on the basis of their social and professional characteristics, as indicated in Table 5.

Women overall are slightly younger, and women of the same age are more often single or divorced than their male counterparts. The

	TOTAL POPULATION	FEMALE POPULATION
AGE	Average age: 34	Average age: 32
SENIORITY	Less than 15 years' service - 56%	Less than 15 years' service - 72%
MARITAL STATUS	Married - 60%; single - 31%; Common law - 5%; divorced - 4%	Married - 46%; single - 38% Common law - 7%; divorced - 7%
FAMILY STATUS (NO. OF CHILDREN)	None - 50%; one or two - 38% three or more - 11%	None - 54%; one or two -41%; three or more - 5%
CONTRACT/CAREER	Contract - 42%	Contract - 60%

TABLE 5. SAMPLE COMPARISONS: MEN AND WOMEN, 1998 [16]

greatest difference is between male and female officers. Females are more often single or divorced with no children, whereas the males are more often married with larger families. With regard to professional criteria, women are more junior in terms of years of service and, accordingly, more likely to be on contract. Furthermore, military life remains largely segregated: women are concentrated primarily in administrative occupations, which is the case, for example, for almost 70 percent of Army women, as opposed to 20 percent of their male counterparts. In the Air Force and Navy, women are no longer a rarity in the technical fields (mechanical, electronics, etc.). Nevertheless, they are still in the minority: 35 percent of female sailors and 20 percent of female airmen are in the technical fields, compared to more than 50 percent for males in both categories. In the case of officers, it is clear that females do not develop in these organizations. In the Army, they constitute only 1 percent of the combat arms officers, compared to 13 percent of the technical and administrative corps and 9 percent of the clerks. We find similar patterns in the other services, where females are virtually absent from the officer corps.

However, a single binary contrast between the sexes is not sociologically sufficient. Distinctions need to be drawn even within the female population (just as with the male population) because the profiles differ particularly in terms of rank, which is not without its impact on their view of being female military personnel.

First, female officers, who are more often career entrants, are on average older, married (to an officer) or single, and half of them have no children. They are practising Catholics, their parents are married, and they are more often only daughters. Their fathers are executives, and their mothers are homemakers. They have studied the arts or sciences at university; their joining the armed forces constituted a professional choice. Second, non-commissioned female members (soldier to master-corporal), all under contract, are young, more often single, and without children. Their boyfriends are more often civilians and in unstable work situations. They come from larger families, and their parents are more likely to be divorced. Their fathers are manual labourers, and their mothers work outside the home. They have a CAP-BEP (college degree) or a high school diploma in administration. They were more often unemployed or in unstable jobs before joining the service. For many, the armed forces offered a way out and no doubt represented an opportunity to get ahead. Third, the population of non-commissioned female officers (sergeant to chief warrant officer) is more heterogeneous, and all the patterns present in the other rank groups are found here. A high proportion of them are unmarried.

In order to understand women's motivations, it is necessary to cross-reference rank and service. For example, non-commissioned officers, particularly in the Air Force and Navy, need to acquire independence quickly after graduation from high school with a view to a specific occupation. Members of the Army indicated that their motivation had existed for several years, with an explicit desire to work in a male environment. They were also more apt to describe themselves as tomboys ("like sailors") in order to substantiate their choice. Finally, the attraction to a military lifestyle was found primarily in the Army and the Navy.

RESULTS AND DISCUSSION

The growing number of women in the French services has come about in recent years as a highly pragmatic goal in response to an unprecedented requirement for personnel in the areas of ORs, volunteers, and, to a lesser extent, officers on contract. In fact, the acceleration in numbers since the late 1990s has been concentrated primarily at the lowest levels in the hierarchy. For the officers, it has owed nothing to the willingness of the military academies to provide access to better positions. Rather, it has been thanks to the market that the women are recruited largely as officers on contract, especially for positions in the legal area and the fields of public relations, teaching, and human resources more generally. Hence, women are kept far from positions that have heavy symbolic "operational" content and that would open the way to greater responsibility. With good reason, the goal of women in the services must be approached with consideration for the ultimate purpose of the institution, namely operational, to the extent that the issue of access to "combat" jobs has been a determining factor in the evolution of the status of women over the past fifty years. Today, the pathway to high command is still held to a very large extent by male hands.

In this regard, the armed forces as an institution does not escape the tendency observed in other areas, whether in the private or public sector, that the arrival of women in most occupations since the 1980s is not synonymous with an egalitarian trend. Discriminatory practices take different forms in the professional and relational spheres. As was apparent from sociologist Sabine Fortino's investigations into the process of gender integration in two organizations in the French public sector,[17] we see in the armed forces the phenomenon of "logic of differential work assignment by gender" reinforced in some areas by "internal gender-determined structuring of occupations". Even where men and women have the same occupation, they do not necessarily perform the same tasks. For example, female naval technicians say that their superiors pressure them to do departmental administrative work. Others, still a minority, are refused a desired place in a department or in a unit. Many others deplore assignments to tasks that are seen as strictly feminine, such as bearing a cushion during a ceremony, working in the cloakroom or in reception at a unit open house, being the female delegate at an official dinner, bearing the responsibility for making coffee. Some report aggressive behaviour by their superiors aimed at putting them on suspension; they cannot afford the slightest mistake, or at least that is what they perceive. They often have to justify the legitimacy of their presence, their professional competence, or even their family choices. They feel that their behaviour is unfairly questioned with respect to, for example, absences or pregnancy, which many of them believe affects their evaluation by misogynistic male superiors.

In terms of relations between the sexes, judging by the most grotesque example of training at the École Spéciale Militaire at Saint-Cyr, the model for the integration of female cadets is one of male-female confrontation. One might even say that it amounts to a war between the sexes launched by the young men and not by the young women's choice, a war that is moreover highly unequal – a handful of young women confronting a hundred or so young men. The males have a variety of tactics that diminish the status of women and make them feel as if they are outsiders, such as pretending that the young women are invisible; treating them with scorn; insulting them; using sexual jokes and sexual innuendo aimed at demeaning women and generally making comments of a sexually suggestive nature. These practices are sustained by a lack of disciplinary action on the part of officers and instructors, virtually all of whom are men. The women must react properly if they are to be accepted by the group because, for many, particularly for young women who are in a small minority in the group, this is primarily a rite of initiation or part of the hazing process.

Clearly, not all of the discrimination is against women. Men and women appear to recognize that women are preferred for some military requirements. Women do receive preferential treatment in some military circumstances. The most frequently cited example is that airwomen are excused more often from night "pick-ups" when the base is on exercise for a week, a circumstance that occurs only every 18 months. Moreover, it is difficult for most of the men to conceive of having military colleagues who are female, even if they are only secretaries. All this must be qualified, however, by stating that this view is far from unanimous. For example, officers who have sailed on mixed warships say that they had no concerns about the effectiveness of their ship during the missions assigned to them.

The fact remains, however, that most women have to analyze and anticipate everything. They must be continually on their guard, on the defensive; they can take nothing for granted – everything must be fought for. All of this raises many reservations, doubts, and even feelings of guilt if, for example, they are away for months at a time, leaving their children with their fathers. And even when they make a special effort, such as to minimize the impact of pregnancy on their duties, they feel such efforts are unappreciated and futile. They may also feel inadequate in their status and role as military personnel when they are pregnant and have to wear civilian clothes, particularly when they have command responsibilities. Their sense is that they are not understood as individuals, but rather are assimilated into a gender-based group of women as defined and regarded by men and reinforced, to some extent, by themselves. They reject a stereotyped image of women, especially one based on the pejorative language which suggests they are part of a movement of "self-deprecation of their gender."

The common goal of virtually all women in the armed forces is to be regarded as soldiers in every respect. However, they do not necessarily agree about the ways to achieve this. The concept of integration does not mean the same thing to all women because, like the male population, women are not a homogeneous group that can be defined in terms of a single dimension. Among the women there are differences in profile, status, and behaviour that are frequently associated with their generation. This is why the issue of women in the armed forces cannot be reduced to a common denominator. Theirs is a pluralistic, heterogeneous population. They do not all have the same prior experiences, characteristics, motivations, career paths, or career prospects; neither do they display the same defence mechanisms to help them get by, nor do they all fight the same battle for social recognition.

It is in this regard that the issue of femininity, which is synonymous with danger and uncertainty for male society, is most revealing. First, it shows to what extent the armed forces as an institution finds it difficult to control, regulate, or manage the balance between uniformity and differentiation. The Navy provides an exemplary case. Alongside official language that describes a trend towards "the normalization" of female roles in the Navy, an embarkation booklet is given to each new woman arriving on a warship. In the second version, which dates from 1999, so-called humorous drawings (which are actually improbable and caricature-like) show a highly sexualized image of women opposite weak men. The women are shown as provocative and the men as victims. Then, the question of their physical makeup and the use of their body reveals disparities and shows that the "hexis corporelle", to use Pierre Bourdieu's expression, explains in part the place to which each aspires within the armed forces and the way in which they perceive their integration. Some personal choices (e.g., makeup, jewellery, hairstyle) differ according to such factors as age, occupation, type of assignment, and branch of service, and each is justified in various ways.

At one end of the range are the women who say they are first and foremost soldiers, who do not make themselves up or wear jewellery. They tend to wear their hair long and pinned up or cut very short; they are primarily young female soldiers assigned to regiments or sailors who are technicians and/or assigned to a warship. They consider themselves integrated from the moment when the men, their male colleagues, stop changing their behaviour in their presence and talk to them as they would to any other soldier – in other words, as they would to a man. They cite examples of vocabulary, forms of address, or topics of conversation. They say that they refuse to be called "Mademoiselle" or "Miss" and that they decline privileges. Some of them ignore pornographic posters, as a way of participating in forms of male socialization, but set limits by, for instance, leaving the men alone during evenings of heavy drinking. The aim here is to claim uniformity in terms of professional equality, to the point of rejecting their femininity, at least during working hours, as they make it a point of honour to draw the distinction between working time (military) and off-hours (civilian), when they become women again.

At the other end are the women who claim that they are first and foremost women: they wear jewellery and makeup and generally wear their hair long and loose; they tend primarily to be airwomen or assigned to staff jobs; they are older and married and have children. For them, while they insist that they are military in every respect, the issue is acceptance of their differences and their complementarities; they are women, not men, in every respect.

Between these two groups lies a part of the sample that is far more heterogeneous, in which the social and professional characteristics are present in almost equal measure, although there is perhaps an over-representation of Army officers and fewer naval officers, and women who wear little or no jewellery. They say they are just as much women as soldiers, they do not regard the two states as incompatible, and they refuse to draw a distinction between the professional and private spheres. Their aim is to be accepted both as soldiers and as women, in other words to be respected in both roles. They reject any imposition on their dignity. They believe that they can be good soldiers without denying their status as women or their femininity.

Most women say that they manage to have nothing to blame themselves for and to avoid any ambiguity related to sexuality. For some, especially the officers, this can lead to developing a shell, which they say they tend to break when they become mothers. Quite simply, they seek to establish good, healthy, professional relationships with their male colleagues, a goal that some say they have achieved at certain times – out on an exercise or on a seagoing assignment, for instance – as these are more conducive to exchanges and thus to enhanced mutual understanding, as well as the fact that everyone is "in the same boat", as it were.

What emerges from this research is the ambiguity of the situation of women in terms of how they view their place. It is by no means rare to encounter, within the same conversation, two positions between a total rejection of any feminine benchmarks (so-called "feminine" values) and also a search for or validation of such benchmarks and of some of these values. The former is an attempt to reject the social characterization of femininity in order to become a soldier like men, and thus to achieve full legitimacy. We are dealing with a phenomenon, described by Danièle Kergoat, of the "syllogism of the subject of female gender,"[18] in the sense that such women have a tendency to downgrade the category of women by removing themselves from it, in a sort of denial of women's group identity. For example, they express a wish to remain in a minority in order to retain the exceptional nature of their choice of profession, and not to overturn everything. They reject the idea of female sections in the military academies. The male benchmark is very much present in the motivation of young women, particularly noticeable in Army women and, to a lesser extent, naval women. These women say they are attracted by the masculine environment, by a masculine profession, and by the idea of working with men, that they are tomboys.

None of this reflects denial of their femininity, but rather a wish to advance it, to discover it or seek it out – to say that they are both soldiers and women, not men. The older ones say that the institution has changed a little since they joined, because women have a different conception of the profession of arms, a complementary notion in a positive sense, for example with regard to the relationship between the personal and professional spheres. This complementarity is also cited by officers with respect to command by drawing on a type of authority that is different but, in their view, equally effective. For others, it is a matter of seeking out the company of other women or at least not feeling isolated. The attitude of the officers from Saint-Cyr at the end of their training for the support arms, as opposed to combat arms, is oriented in this way, for example, in addition to the fact that they do not wish to be confronted with a world that is excessively hostile to their integration. Their primary desire is to achieve professional credibility. Army officer cadets say that they like having female instructors, particularly when it comes to constructing their own destiny and finding accessible, credible role models. Finally, some elements of militancy were found; for example, young naval NCOs say that they want to try the officer competition, among other things, to fight for the cause of women in the Navy.

CONCLUSION

The results show the extent to which the issue of the role of women in the armed forces in France focuses around two key interdependent terms: integration and conflict. It would thus appear that the integration function is the one that receives the primary emphasis, though all-too-often hypothetical. The aim, especially for younger women assigned to operational units, is to deal with rejection, isolation, and unhealthy attitudes–held primarily, but not exclusively, by males. Women furthermore are obliged, far more often than men, to adjust, to make concessions, and to stifle certain traits in their personality. The situations that have been described have appeared as interpersonal relationships that often produce conflict, not only between men and women but also among the women themselves. Women feel that they are confronting an identity conflict between, on the one hand, a personal and social identity (identity as a woman) and, on the other hand, a professional identity (identity as a member of the profession of arms); male benchmarks remain central in both images and practices. In fact, the problem for them, as a gender-defined group, is to gain acceptance, to be integrated into a masculine environment that was closed to them at the outset and often remains hostile.

Clearly, this study is limited by its exclusive focus on the female population. But, given the paucity of sociological studies on this topic, this was necessary in order to build a solid basis for future research. That research will approach the subject from the perspectives of men, of the armed forces as an institution, and of social relationships between the sexes, with a view to understanding the issues involved in the "feminization" of military practices, the virile benchmark, the place of family life in the profession of arms, the image of the leader, and, more generally, of command, modes of military socialization, and recruiting.

It is hoped that this chapter has cast some light on both the barriers that confront women in the French Armed Forces, along with some suggestions through which conflictual elements may be overcome. To be sure, effective human resource policies are necessary to make women's transition and integration into all service environments less problematic. These policies should recognize that women are not necessarily a homogenous group and there are, therefore, no magic bullets to eliminate the inherent conflicts for women. Notwithstanding, the obstacles that French women have faced, and continue to face, are universal among armed forces that employ women in uniform; so are many of the institutional changes that are necessary to successfully overcoming them.

NOTES

1   For a fuller discussion, see Katia Sorin, *Femmes en armes: une place introuvable? Le cas de la féminisation de l'armée française*, (Paris: L'Harmattan, 2003).

2   For a general presentation on the French Armed Forces, see Boëne Bernard and Martin Michel Louis, "France: In the Throes of Epoch-Making Change," in T*he Postmodern Military: Armed Forces after the Cold War*, Charles Moskos, Williams John Allen, and David Segal, eds. (New York: Oxford University Press, 2000), 51-79.

3   See especially studies by the sociologist Emmanuel Reynaud: *Les femmes dans l'armée: situation actuelle et perspectives* (Paris: Fondation pour les études de défense nationale, 1986); *Maternité et activité professionnelle des femmes. Le cas de la marine et de la Gendarmerie* (Paris: Fondation pour les études de défense nationale/Secrétariat d'État chargé des droits des femmes, 1988); *Les femmes, la violence et l'armée. Essai sur la féminisation des armées* (Paris: Fondation pour les études de défense nationale, 1988); and Michel Martin, "From Periphery to Center. Women in the French Military", Armed Forces and Society, vol. 8, no. 2, 1982: 303-333.

4   For example, Isabelle Burot-Besson and Nadia Chellig, *Les enjeux de la féminisation du corps des médecins des armées*, report, LADEC/C2SD, 2001; Guy Friedmann, Leila Benkara, and Daniel Loriot, Métiers de la défense, les choix des femmes. *Agencements identitaires et mixité des emplois de l'armée de Terre*, report, ralentir travaux !/C2SD, 2001; Pascale Trompette, Jean Saglio, and Serge Dufoulon, *La différence perdue. La féminisation de l'équipage du Montcalm, report*, CRISTO-CNRS/C2SD, 1998.

5   For example, R. Laroche, ed., *Les mesures de soutien nécessaires aux personnels militaires féminins engagés sur les théâtres d'opérations extérieures et à leurs familles* (Paris: Ministère de la Défense, Service de santé des armées, 2000); *Étude relative à la féminisation de la Gendarmerie* (Paris: Direction générale de la Gendarmerie nationale, Service des ressources humaines, 1999); *Les femmes militaires. Repères socio-démographiques et aspects sociologiques* (Paris, Observatoire Social de la Défense, 2000).

6   Goffman Erving, *Stigmate. Les usages sociaux du corps* (Paris, Ed. de minuit, 1963).

7   Some fifteen interviews were conducted with male personnel, most of them sailors, in addition to a large number of informal discussions.

8   With the exception of air medical escorts (convoyeuses de l'air), who serve under contract. They are nurses who have a specialization in aeronautical medicine and in air

medevac and hold officer rank.

9   For example, the maximum recruiting quotas are 5 percent for the Special Military Academy (Army), 10 percent for the Naval Academy, and 20 percent for the Air Force Academy. All occupational specialties or services are subject to quotas, with the exception of administration for Army non-commissioned officers, for example.

10   This is a new category created in the wake of the suspension of conscription: it is a one-year contract that can be renewed up to four times.

11   Source: Direction de la fonction militaire et du personnel civil.

12   Even though their percentage will probably increase fairly rapidly over the next ten years, to the extent that the most recent recruitment figures show that women constitute over half the cadets.

13   Thus, resource availability is calculated as follows: 100 percent of an age group of boys and only 15 percent of an age group of girls.

14   Preparatory classes in "special mathematics" for the Air Force and Navy, where women are already in a minority.

15   École spéciale militaire (Army), École de l'air (Air Force), École navale (Navy).

16   Most of the data concerned the Army, the Air Force and the Navy. The data are taken from l'Observatoire Social de la Défense and the military personnel branch of each service.

17   Sabine Fortino, *La mixité au travail* (Paris: La Dispute, 2002).

18   Quoted by Fortino, ibid., 172.

HARASSMENT IN THE MILITARY: CROSS-NATIONAL COMPARISONS

NICOLA J. HOLDEN AND KAREN D. DAVIS

INTRODUCTION

Over the past several decades, the reduction or elimination of various forms of discrimination against social groups and individuals has become both a social concern and a legal issue, especially in democratic societies. One of the more odious forms of discrimination is harassment. In 1979 in the United States, for example, Catharine MacKinnon made a convincing argument that sexual harassment constituted unlawful discrimination within the meaning of the Equal Protection Clause of the 14th Amendment to the US Constitution and relevant United States statutes.[1] Since that time, harassment has received greater attention as a barrier to the status of women and members of minority groups in employment organizations and in the labour force overall. As well, harassment is increasingly seen to result in excessive costs to organizations and to be both an impediment to performance and a significant consumer of resources associated with processing, investigating, and litigating harassment complaints.

Harassment is a particularly salient issue within military organizations, as women and minority groups continue to be significantly under-represented; their small numbers and their relative newcomer status make them vulnerable to discrimination and harassment. Consequently, countering harassment has been demanding significant resources and attention as Western military organizations face increased pressure to effectively integrate representative numbers of women and men from national populations that are becoming more diverse. In addition, militaries rely more and more on women and members of visible minority and Aboriginal groups to fill their ranks, rendering the recruitment, retention, and optimum employment of these members important to the success of the organization – from the perspectives of both operations and public accountability.

Throughout the 1980s and 1990s, a number of policies, programs, and training initiatives aimed at reducing the incidence of harassment were introduced into the Canadian Forces. Surveys were designed and administered to determine the experiences and perceptions of military members and civilian employees concerning unwanted sexual and harassing behaviour, thus providing a measure of the effectiveness of those policies and programs. The initial surveys and the resultant baseline data on incidence of harassment were followed by similar or identical surveys. Hence, over time and in specific Western-style militaries, indicators as to whether the reported rates of harassment have remained stable, decreased, or increased, have begun to be established. This chapter offers a comparative analysis of case studies, based on the results of eight surveys administered within the militaries of four Western nations: Australia, Canada, New Zealand, and the United States.[2]

Australia, Canada, and the United States have been measuring the incidence of harassment in their military organizations for over a decade, and New Zealand has more recently implemented such a monitoring process. While much of the impetus for the development of harassment policies and programs and the subsequent measurement of the impact of implementing them are embedded within national laws and legislation,[3] these nations do share cultural characteristics that make comparison meaningful. Their respective militaries assign considerable significance to military traditions and practices that are heavily influenced by a predominantly white heterosexual male culture and a Judeo-Christian tradition. Consequently, the experiences of these nations in introducing women (and non-Caucasian or non-heterosexual members of their societies) into their militaries also have many similarities. Nevertheless, the specific context for the measurement of harassment, including stage of policy development, effectiveness and frequency of training, and the cultures of both nations and services, do vary and thus they affect the design, administration, analysis, and results of surveys. In most cases, survey efforts have been directed toward measuring the impact of centralized harassment policy and programs on the incidence of harassment in the military organizations. However, for a variety of definitional and methodological reasons, direct comparisons across the various militaries cannot always be made. Thus, we begin by providing a background discussion of the most relevant issues affecting these cross-national comparisons.

DEFINITIONS AND METHODOLOGIES:

Defining Harassment

While the case studies use many identical and near-identical questionnaire items and share considerable agreement as to what types of behaviour constitute harassment, they also vary in their definitions of harassment. Many of the surveys include such a definition or a pre-amble in reference to harassment, which assists both respondents and interpreters of the data. Some questionnaires provide a list of harass-ment behaviours; others ask respondents directly if they have been harassed. Such variations in approach influence the results. For exam-ple, Culbertson et al. found that asking "respondents directly if they have been sexually harassed provides a much different and lower rate of sexual harassment than if respondents are asked if they have experi-enced any of a series of categories of unwanted sexual behaviours and a rate is calculated based on those responses."[4]   Researchers in Australia, Canada, and the United States used not only definitions of the various forms of harassment but also a list of behaviours.

For research purposes, the range of behaviours used in describing and interpreting harassment, discrimination, or indicators of a positive working "climate" also varies within and across nations. The United States 1996 *Armed Forces Equal Opportunity Survey*, for example, lists a range of 42 behaviours as "incidents" with the potential to affect respondents due to their race and ethnicity. Harassment surveys in Canada, New Zealand, and the United States list similar behaviours in the context of sex/gender harassment.[5] Other behaviours used in the equal opportunity survey are similar to experiences defined as "abuse of authority" in the 1992 and 1998 CF harassment questionnaires.[6] The United States *Navy Equal Opportunity and Sexual Harassment Survey* (NEOSH) also asks respondents to indicate if they have experienced a range of presented behaviours, including negative comments, offensive jokes, and physical assault, "because of your *racial or ethnic group*" or "because of your *gender*" and subsequently reports responses as incident rates of racial or ethnic and gender discrimination. Although none of these surveys identify the behaviours as harassment per se, the intent and name of the survey itself pre-defined the behaviours presented (e.g., as either an "equal opportunity" or "harassment" survey).

Although a distinction between harassment and discrimination is implied by definition within the various surveys, this distinction is much less clear in practice. In fact, as indicated earlier, harassment can be understood as one form of discrimination rather than as a unique occurrence, behaviour, or process. Also, if an overall positive work "climate" is the goal, the definitions become much less important than the experience itself, the impact on individuals, or ultimately, the impact on the effectiveness and/or productivity of the group.

SAMPLING AND RESPONSE RATES

Harassment surveys have been administered within specific environments (Navy, Army, or Air Force), across defence forces as a whole (Regular and Reserve Force personnel), and across defence departments (military and civilian personnel). Questionnaires were administered to random stratified samples, frequently including an over-sampling of particular member sub-groups (e.g., women, senior officers). Response rates are generally reported in their entirety – in some cases by officer/enlisted, rank group (e.g., junior officer, senior officer), or gender. In some cases, under- and over-representation within particular sub-groups have been accounted for through statistical weighting of the sample prior to analysis.

PARAMETERS OF REPORTED HARASSMENT

The time frame over which harassment was reported varied somewhat between nations and surveys. However, there was much more variation in terms of the specified location of the harassment, the activity during which the harassment occurred, and the status of the alleged offender. The most common time period for self-reporting of harassment was the previous year or last 12 months. In some cases, however, respondents were asked to report incidents within the previous two-year period or incidents that were occurring at the time of the survey. Each country had a different set of contextual parameters for self-reporting of harassment.

The 2000 Australian Defence Force (ADF) questionnaire was perhaps the most detailed, asking about "situations involving… military personnel (on or off duty) (on or off base/unit) (including trainees, recruits, cadets), and/or civilian employees (e.g. contractors, Defence civilians)".[7] The 1995 New Zealand Defence Force (NZDF) questionnaire specified "service environment, including social occasions", while the 1998 CF questionnaire specified, "by a service member, *in the workplace or in matters/events related to work* [emphasis original]".[8] The 1995 U.S. Department of Defense (DoD) survey made a distinction, in two separate questions, between uninvited and unwanted sexual attention experienced "from someone AT WORK while serving in the active-duty military [emphasis original]" and "from someone where you work in the active-duty military".[9] In all cases, respondents were free to report harassment occurring at any time in a 24-hour period, in recognition of the nature of military service – that is, 24 hours per day, every day, with members living, working, and socializing in the same environment. In some cases, however, details of the physical environment, the status of the alleged offender, or whether the respondent was actually on the job at the time of the reported harassment were indicated. These contextual differences, among others, place some limitations on making direct, specific comparisons but do allow general-case comparisons.

QUESTIONNAIRE CONTENT AND ORGANIZATION

The content of the questions and the organization of the question-naire were also considered for comparative analysis. Although there is little consistency across case studies in the categories or labels used to organize, present, and prioritize harassment and discrimi-nation, there is considerable similarity in the types of behaviour determined to constitute harassment. In the CF 1998 survey, questionnaire items asked respondents about their experience with four separate types of harassment, including sexual and personal harassment, abuse of authority, and hazing. All surveys had at least one section on sexual harassment. The ADF 1995 and 2000 and the U.S. DoD Form A 1995 surveys included the Sexual Experiences Questionnaire (SEQ),[10] a behaviourally anchored scale, to measure five types of sexual harassment: gender harassment, seductive behaviour, sexual bribery, sexual coercion, and sexual assault. A comparative analysis of the 1995 ADF and U.S. DoD SEQ administrations concluded that the more serious the behaviour, the more likely that the ADF had reported a similar or lower incident rate than the U.S. DoD.[11]

Although standard definitions of harassment do not exist across nations, substantial common ground in survey items indicates that there is considerable agreement as to what types of behaviour constitute harassment. In total, eight behaviours were presented with identical or near-identical wording in the CF 1998, NZDF 1995, and U.S. DoD Form A 1995 surveys, and four identical or near-identical behaviours were used in the CF 1998, NZDF 1995, and U.S. DoD Form A 1995 surveys. The ADF 2000, CF 1998, and NZDF 1995 surveys presented seven common perceived bases of personal harassment (religion, skin colour, etc.) to their respondents in a separate question. In addition, a number of survey items were shared across two to four of the militaries compared; for example, the US 1995 survey and the CF 1998 survey share 28 common items; the U.S. 1995, CF 1998, and ADF 2000 share 15 common items; the US 1995, CF 1998, and NZDF 1995 share 14 common items; and the US 1995, CF 1998, NZDF 1995, and ADF 2000 share 10 common items.

It should be noted, however, that the common items and categories discussed in this paper were rarely presented in the same order or within the same context across the nations surveyed. For example, both the 1988 DoD survey and the 1989 U.S. Naval Equal Opportunity and Sexual Harassment (NEOSH) survey listed the same eight categories of sexually harassing behaviour, but the DoD survey presented behaviours from the most serious to the least serious, and the NEOSH presented them in reverse order. Similarly, the eight shared behaviour descriptors of harassment appeared in a similar order in the U.S. DoD and CF surveys but in a quite different order in the NZDF survey. The U.S. DoD survey described these behaviours as "unwanted, uninvited"; the NZDF survey described them as "unwelcome and/or offensive"; and the CF survey simply listed the behaviours without a preceding descriptor. The ADF and CF used similar, but not identical, scales to measure frequency of harassment experience, while the NZDF survey asked respondents to specify frequency as well as whether the harassment affected them and whether it was observed or experienced. The U.S. DoD Form A asked respondents to "mark all that apply" but did not ask for an indication of frequency.

ANALYSIS AND REPORTING

Finally, there are differences in the way the comparison nations have analyzed the survey data and reported the results. For example, when members were asked how they responded to harassment, three nations presented an item reading, "I ignored the behaviour or did nothing"; however, each nation reported the output data in a different manner. Canada reported the results by female/male, Australia reported the result as a whole, and the U.S. did not report the result at all in their formal publications, although they asked the question. Initial analyses of the ADF 1995 and U.S. DoD 1995 administrations of the SEQ also yielded variations in reported data; however, Simmons' 1998 re-analysis[12] reported the percentage of women and men experiencing each of 24 behaviours, thus facilitating a comparison of the results in the two countries.

Although we have dealt at some length with the variations in definitions and methodologies across comparison nations, we still believe that the case analyses and comparisons within nations are worth reporting. We also believe that, despite study differences, the trend lines lead to some fairly clear conclusions, which we provide at the end of this chapter. We now move to consider individual national data comparisons.

AUSTRALIAN DEFENCE FORCE: SEXUAL HARASSMENT

In 1995, *The Australian Defence Force: Career and Family Study* asked both male and female members questions pertaining to

sexual harassment, replicating a 1987 study that has been administered only to female members. Harassment was defined as follows:

Gender and/or sexual harassment covers behaviours which range
from annoying verbal comments to embarrassing, unwanted
pressure to have sexual contact with a work superior often with the
threat or implication that your career, job or course assessment will
suffer if you refuse. Gender and/or sexual harassment is a problem
if it makes you feel uncomfortable, uneasy at work, singled out for
unwanted attention, or if it makes doing your job difficult.

The study included 40 questions related to sexual harassment,
including items comprising the SEQ[13] and a series of questions
about a selected experience of sexual harassment. Respondents were
asked to indicate which of the 24 behaviours comprising the SEQ
they had experienced in the past 12 months. The situation could
have involved military personnel (on or off duty, on or off the base
or unit), civilian employees and contractors employed in the
workplace, or some combination of these factors.

The questionnaire was sent to a representative sample of 5,000
regular force men and women up to the rank of Lieutenant-Colonel
and equivalent. The sample was stratified by service, gender, and
rank. Women and senior-rank levels were over-sampled to ensure
adequate numbers for the analysis, and the sample was weighted to
be representative of the total ADF population.[14] The overall
response rate was 62 percent.

Comparison of the 1995 results to the survey conducted in 1987
found that the incidence of all types of sexual harassment for
servicewomen had declined.[15] Initial analysis of the behaviours
described in the SEQ, however, found that women "are several times
more likely than men to experience most of the harassing
behaviours, but up to 60 per cent of men described offensive

sex-related behaviours in their work environment".[16] Comparable data from the 1987 and 1995 surveys, aggregated for analysis as "gender harassment/hostile workplace", "unwanted sexual attention", and "sexual coercion", are presented in Figure 1.

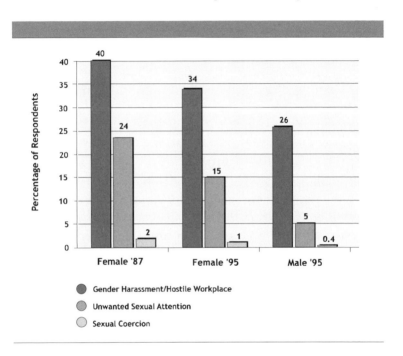

FIGURE 1:   1987 AND 1995 ADF CAREER AND FAMILY STUDY (REGULAR
            FORCE): SELF-REPORT INCIDENTS OCCURRING, FOR TYPE
            OF HARASSMENT INDICATED, AT TIME OF SURVEY.

EXPERIENCES OF UNACCEPTABLE BEHAVIOUR IN THE ADF

The *Survey of Your Experiences of Unacceptable Behaviour in the Military* was administered in October 2000, using the SEQ to measure the incidence of harassment behaviours. The survey defined harassment as follows: "Unwanted sex-related behaviour is sex-related talk and/or behaviour that was unwanted, uninvited, and in which you did not participate willingly." It was sent to a sample of 5,000 ADF personnel, stratified by service and rank. Female ADF members were over-sampled to comprise 50 percent (2,500) of the sample, and male members comprised the other 50 percent (2,500) of the sample. The overall response rate to the survey was 47.2 percent. The female response rate was higher than that of males (52.8 percent versus 41.6 percent), while the Air Force and Army response rates were higher than that of the Navy (53.9 percent, 51.3 percent, and 31.2 percent, respectively).[17]

Respondents were asked to identify behaviours observed during the past 12 months –while they were on or off duty and on or off the base or unit – that involved military personnel, including trainees, recruits, cadets, and civilian employees.[18] Overall, 77.3 percent of female and 63.6 percent of male respondents indicated that they had experienced at least one of the behaviours examined by the SEQ.[19] Comparable data is not available to determine if the sexual harassment incident rates measured by the SEQ have increased, decreased, or remained stable in comparison to the 1987 and 1995 ADF surveys.

The survey also measured experience of unacceptable workplace behaviour on the basis of 14 items ranging from teasing to harassment based on skin colour, religion, age, etc. Overall, 81.9 percent of female respondents and 73.3 percent of male respondents reported having observed at least one of these behaviours in the previous 12 months, with 33.6 percent of females and 16.7 percent of males indicating that the behaviours were unwanted.[20] What did the others indicate?

THE CANADIAN FORCES: PERSONAL HARASSMENT

In 1992, the CF administered a personal harassment survey, which measured the frequency of personal harassment occurrences over the previous 12 months. It was aimed at evaluating the effectiveness of personal-harassment policy, and questions were based on the following definitions:

> *Personal Harassment* – (excluding sexual) an unsolicited behaviour by an individual that is directed at or is offensive to another individual; that is based on personal characteristics including, for example, race, religion, sex, physical character- istics, or mannerisms; and that a reasonable person ought to have known would be unwelcome", "*Sexual Harassment* – a type of personal harassment that has a sexual purpose or is of a sexual nature including, but not limited to, touching, leer- ing, lascivious remarks and the display of pornographic mate- rial", and "*Abuse of Authority* – the misuse of authority to undermine, sabotage, or otherwise interfere with the career of another individual including, but not limited to, intimida- tion, threats, blackmail, coercion, or unfairness in the distri- bution of work assignments, in the provision of training or promotional opportunities, in the completion of perform- ance evaluations, or in the provision of job references."

Approximately 5,700 Regular Force members, of a stratified random sample (females were over-sampled by 20%), were asked if they felt they had experienced personal harassment, sexual harassment, or abuse of authority and were also given a list of behaviours that could be considered harassing behaviour. Of the almost 73% who responded, 26.2 percent of women and 2 percent of men believed they had been subjected to sexual harassment; 32.6 percent of women and 19.4 percent of men believed they had been subjected to personal harassment; and 31.5 percent of women and 28.9 percent of men felt they had been subjected to abuse of authority while performing CF duties during the past 12 months.[21]   Are these absolute or relative?

A more refined follow-up harassment survey in 1998, which replicated many of the questions asked in 1992, addressed four types of harassment. These included personal harassment (excluding sexual), sexual harassment, abuse of authority, and hazing. Definitions for personal and sexual harassment, and abuse of authority were almost identical to those presented in the 1992 survey. Hazing was defined as any activity that is part of an initiation ceremony or rite of passage that offends, demeans, belittles, or humiliates those who participate; it might include, but is not limited to, bullying or cruel horseplay.

The 1998 survey was administered to a stratified random sample of 2,290 Regular and Reserve Force personnel and 2,340 CF personnel undergoing qualification and pre-qualification training, including undergraduate officer candidates at the Royal Military College of Canada. The response rates were 48 percent for the Regular Force, 38 percent for the Reserves, and 38 percent for the training population. While the time frame for incidents remained the same as in the 1992 survey (12 months), the environment was expanded in 1998 to include the location of the harassment more specifically: in the workplace (CF only) or while performing CF duties, on Department of National Defence (DND) property at an organized section/unit social event or at the mess, or off DND property.

For the Regular Force, "39% of women and 24% of men in the CF had experienced one or more of the four types of harassment examined."[22] For the Reserve personnel, about "30% of women and 20% of men reported experiencing any of the four types of harassment in the last 12 months."[23] Within the training sample, 28 percent of women and 16 percent of men reported having experienced some form of harassment in the past 12 months. A comparison of the results for the Regular Force from 1992 to 1998 shows a decline in the incidence of abuse of authority, personal harassment, and sexual harassment. The most notable decline for women was in the rate of sexual harassment, from 26 percent in 1992 to 14 percent in 1998. Comparable data from the 1992 and 1998 survey administrations are presented in Figure 2. The incidence of harassment generally decreased for men as well, except for a possible "error variance"-type increase in sexual harassment.

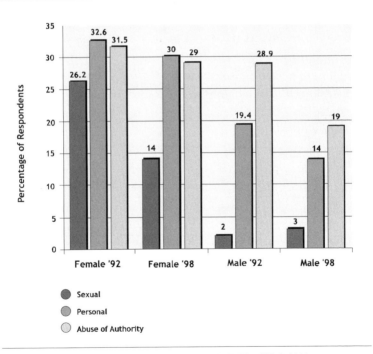

SOURCE: CF (REGULAR) PERSONAL HARASSMENT SURVEY, 1992 & 1998.

FIGURE 2:   SELF-REPORTED INCIDENCE OF HARASSMENT IN THE WORKPLACE AND/OR WHILE PERFORMING DUTIES (1992) AND/OR INVOLVING ACTIVITIES RELATED TO WORK OUTSIDE OF THE WORKPLACE (1998), PREVIOUS 12 MONTHS (WOMEN/MEN).

NEW ZEALAND:
INCIDENCE AND MANAGEMENT OF HARASSMENT

The 1995 survey, created by the NZDF to investigate incidence and management of harassment issues, was adapted from the CF Personal Harassment Questionnaire and the U.S. DoD Harassment Survey. In this initial administration, 12 of the 14 perceived bases of harassment (religion, race, etc.) presented to NZDF respondents were identical to those in the Canadian questionnaire, and 8 of the 10 potentially unwelcome or offensive behaviours presented were identical or nearly identical to those presented in the United States and Canadian surveys. However, the NZDF survey did not provide either a preamble in reference to harassment or a definition.

The intent of the survey was to seek information about the occurrence of general and sexual harassment, the effects of harassment, commanders/supervisors' actions and responses to harassment, and the characteristics of harassees and alleged perpetrators. Respondents were asked if they had either observed or personally experienced harassing or sexually harassing behaviours over the past 12 months within the Service environment, including social occasions, and if the observation of harassment had affected them. The survey incorporated two different methods for determining occurrence rates of sexual harassment: one asked respondents directly if they had been sexually harassed; the other provided a series of categories of unwanted sexual behaviours that were aggregated to provide an incident rate.

The survey was sent out to 10 percent of the military and civilian populations. "Although a single standardized questionnaire was developed, some customization was used to reflect single Service and HQ [headquarters] NZDF requirements and references, such as ranks and Corps/Branches, which differ between services".[24] Approximately 1,160 people were sent the survey and the response rate was about 80 percent.

For each Service and the headquarters of the NZDF, the results were analyzed separately. Common themes emerged: results from the individual Services consistently indicated that proportionately, females experienced greater levels of general harassment based on sex, harassment of a sexual nature, and harassment based on physical characteristics. Also, proportionately more women than men reported experiencing sexually harassing behaviours, with approximately 30 percent of women having experienced sexual teasing and between 13 and 20 percent (depending on the service) having experienced unwelcome or offensive touching, leaning over, or pinching.[25]

UNITED STATES 1995 DEPARTMENT OF DEFENSE SEXUAL HARASSMENT STUDY

This survey consisted of three different forms. Form A was replicated from the 1988 DoD-wide survey that produced the first baseline data on sexual harassment in the active-duty Services, facilitating the comparison of the self-reported sexual harassment incident rates from 1988 and 1995. This form was sent to 30,756 personnel in 1995; 13,599 (46 percent) completed the survey.

Results indicated a decline in respondents' self-reports of sexual harassment from 1988 to 1995. In 1988, 64 percent of active duty military women and 17 percent of active duty military men reported experiencing "unwanted, uninvited sexual attention" while at work in the year prior to the survey, as compared to 55 percent of women and 14 percent of men reporting this in 1995 (Figure 3).

In 1995, Form B contained a list of 25 behaviours comprising the SEQ and also expanded the environment in which the harassment had taken place (i.e., at work or off the base or installation). Form B also measured respondents' perceptions of the complaint process and training. This form was sent to 50,394 personnel; 28,296

(58 percent) responded.[26] Seventy-eight percent of women and 38 percent of men indicated they had experienced one or more of the behaviours listed in the survey during the previous 12 months. The authors of the 1995 survey report noted, "when asked whether they considered any of the behaviours they experienced to be sexual harassment, about one-third of women and nearly three-quarters of men said that none of their experiences constituted harassment".[27]

UNITED STATES 1996 ARMED FORCES EQUAL OPPORTUNITY SURVEY (AFEOS)

The AFEOS was developed for the purpose of gaining a better understanding of service members' perceptions and experiences with respect to fair treatment and equal opportunity.[28] The method of assessing personal experiences of racial or ethnic insensitivity, harassment, and discrimination paralleled the method used in the 1995 Armed Forces Sexual Harassment Survey to measure experiences of harassment. Specifically, respondents were asked how often they had experienced any of 42 "various incidents" during the past 12 months. In addition, they were asked to indicate if the described incident or behaviour was perpetrated by "military personnel (on or off duty, on or off installation) and/or service/DoD civilian employees (on or off installation)", or "civilians in the local community around an installation". Several of the first 15 behaviours and incidents presented were similar in nature to the behaviours presented as "unwanted" and "uninvited" sexual attention in the 1995 DoD Sexual Harassment Study, but were raised this time in the context of race and ethnicity. In the case of the other 26 incidents, respondents were also asked if they believed their race or ethnicity was a related factor.

The 1996 AFEOS was administered from September 1996 to February 1997 to all ranks in the Army, Navy, Marine Corps, Air Force, and Coast Guard. The target population was a random sample that took into account the complexity of the population, including different racial and ethnic groups, rank, Service, gender, and geographic location. The survey questionnaire was sent to 76,754 personnel, and the usable return rate was 53 percent.

This questionnaire itself did not make explicit reference to racial or ethnic discrimination; instead, respondents were asked whether they had experienced specific incidents or behaviours. Overall, 81 percent of junior enlisted, 76 percent of senior enlisted, and 67 percent of officers indicated that in the previous year they or their family had experienced at least one of 42 potential incidents related to racial or ethnic harassment or discrimination. Although members of all racial and ethnic groups perceived insensitivity, harassment, and discrimination, members of minority racial and ethnic groups (Black, Hispanic, Asian/Pacific Islander, and Native Americans/Alaskan Natives) indicated they encountered more of these types of problems than did White respondents. Women and men were equally likely to report experience of at least one of ten behaviours identified as an "offensive encounter" (66 percent and 64 percent, respectively) – 10 behaviours that most closely parallelled the "unwanted" and "uninvited" behaviours described in the 1995 DoD Sexual Harassment Survey. Although there were variations in proportions of women and men reporting an "offensive encounter" among different racial or ethnic groups, over-all, junior enlisted members were generally most likely to report "offensive encounters" (74 percent), followed by senior enlisted (67 percent) and officers (49 percent).[29]

UNITED STATES NAVAL EQUAL OPPORTUNITY AND SEXUAL HARASSMENT SURVEY

The NEOSH survey was administered in the Navy every other year between 1989 and 1999. The sexual harassment portion of the survey consisted of three parts: "perceptions about sexual harassment, the forms and frequencies, and the actions and effects resulting from sexual harassment experiences"[30] Respondents were asked, "During the past year, have you been sexually harassed while on duty?" and, "During the past year, have you been sexually harassed on base or ship while off duty?" Harassment was defined as follows.

> Sexual harassment is a form of sex discrimination that involves unwelcome sexual advances, requests for sexual favours, and other verbal or physical conduct of a sexual nature when: 1) submission to or rejection of such conduct is made either explicitly or implicitly a term or condition of a person's job, pay or career, or 2) submission to or rejection of such conduct by a person is used as a basis for career or employment decisions affecting that person, or 3) such conduct interferes with an individual's performance or creates an intimidating, hostile, or offensive environment. Any person in a supervisory or command position who uses or condones implicit or explicit sexual behaviour to control, influence, or affect the career, pay or job of a military member or civilian employee is engaging in sexual harassment. Similarly, any military member or civilian employee who makes deliberate or repeated unwelcome verbal comments, gestures, or physical contact of a sexual nature is also engaging in sexual harassment. Both men and women can be victims of sexual harassment; both women and men can be sexual harassers; people can sexually harass persons of their own sex.

Stratified random samples of active duty enlisted and officer personnel were identified for all surveys to allow for comparison of data over the years. Response rates were 60 percent in 1989, 48 percent in 1991, 41 percent in 1993, 40 percent in 1995, 45 percent in 1997, and 30 percent in 1999/2000. Before analysis, "post-stratification weighting by paygrade, gender, and racial/ ethnic group was performed to make the respondents representative of their populations in the Navy". [31]

In the 1989 survey, 42 percent of enlisted women and 26 percent of female officers indicated they had been sexually harassed during the one-year survey period while on duty or on base or ship while off duty. In comparison, 4 percent of enlisted men and 1 percent of male officers reported having been sexually harassed during the same period.[32] A comparison of the results of the 1989 and 1991 surveys turned up a statistically significant increase in the percentage of female officers and enlisted men who reported having been harassed. The 1991 survey found 44 percent of enlisted women and 33 percent of female officers indicating they had been sexually harassed during the one-year period, and 8 percent of enlisted men and 2 percent male officers reported experiencing sexually harassing behaviour.[33]

By 1997, survey findings were significantly lower than the 1989 and 1991 findings for enlisted women and female officers. Twenty-three percent of enlisted women and 13 percent of female officers reported experiencing sexually harassing behaviour, an absolute decrease of 21 percent for enlisted women and 20 percent for female officers over the six-year period 1991 to 1997. The self-report incident rate for male officers declined and remained steady at 1 percent for the 1995 and 1997 surveys, while incident rates for male enlisted decreased to 3 percent in 1995 and remained at 3 percent in 1997. Responses to the 1999/2000 NEOSH reflect a lower percentage of respondents reporting experiences of harassment in the past 12 months compared to previous baseline rates, and there was a significant decline among female officers reporting sexual harassment by senior supervisors.[34]

The 1995, 1997, and 1999/2000 NEOSH also asked respondents about experiences of racial or ethnic and gender discrimination during the previous 12 months. Analysis of responses by White (Caucasian), Black (Afro-Americans), and Hispanic respondents indicates that Black enlisted respondents are most likely to report experiences of racial or ethnic discrimination (41 percent in 1995, 34 percent in 1997), and White officers are least likely to report racial or ethnic discrimination (5 percent in 1995 and 1997). Enlisted women are most likely to report experience of gender discrimination (43 percent in 1995 and 36 percent in 1997), and male officers are least likely to report experience of gender discrimination (4 percent in 1995, 5 percent in 1997). Overall, experiences of discrimination declined among all personnel from 1995 to 1997, with the exception of male officers, whose self-reports reflected a slight increase in gender discrimination. However, initial results of the 1999/2000 NEOSH indicate that racial minorities had not experienced a decline in certain racial discrimination behaviours, and approximately one third of enlisted women and female officers continued to report gender discrimination.[35]

DISCUSSION AND CONCLUSIONS

The results of the various forms of harassment experienced by serving members, as presented above, show trends that are both common to all the nations/militaries studied and some that are specific to the individual militaries concerned. First of all, there seems to be general agreement across nations/militaries as to what constitutes harassment, and the incidence of some forms of harassment has been sufficiently high as to represent a significant problem for all of the militaries studied. Regardless of variations and interpretations, the most recent results from each of the four nations indicate that the forms of sexual harassment most and least commonly experienced are similar in each nation. Of those who reported experiencing harassment, up to 86 percent identified harassment in the form of jokes, comments, teasing, questions, and story-telling (defined variously as "repeatedly told sexual stories or offensive jokes" [ADF 1995]; "sexual teasing, jokes, remarks" [CF 1998, U.S. DoD, 1995]; "sexual teasing, jokes, remarks or questions" [NZDF 1995]). On the other hand, actual or attempted rape, sexual assault, and violence were the least likely to be reported. Although incident rates in this area were quite low, ranging from less than 1.0 percent to 3.7 percent, all nations reported some.

Reported harassment incident rates varied considerably, depending upon the type of harassment being measured, demographic characteristics of the respondent, such as sex and military rank when the survey was administered, and the nation. At one end of the spectrum, 0.4 per cent of male respondents in the ADF in 1994 reported experience of "sexual coercion", while 64 per cent of female military respondents in the United States in 1988 reported experiences of "unwanted, uninvited sexual attention". The available data consistently show that proportionately more women than men are subjected to various forms of harassment.

On the positive side, the above analysis indicates that, where longitudinal studies have been done, results show an overall decrease in the reported incident rates of harassment, for both women and men, throughout the 1990s.[36] Overall absolute decreases in reported incident rates of harassment could be due to a number of factors, including greater emphasis on harassment-prevention programs, the creation and implementation of anti-harassment policies, and visible commitment by senior leadership to eradicate harassment from the military environment. On the other hand, lower rates of reported harassment may result from fear of the consequences of reporting or lack of confidence that military leadership will effectively and fairly address harassment in the work environment.

In any case, surveys of randomly sampled members are likely to produce a more realistic picture of harassment than are harassment complaints only. While issues such as response rates and respondents' perceptions regarding confidentiality and anonymity are a concern, survey administration offers more reliable data than complaint mechanisms that place the burden for eradicating harassment on potentially vulnerable members of the organization rather than on all levels of leadership, where it belongs. We would recommend that these surveys be continued and that efforts continue to make the data directly comparable across nations/militaries. This would provide the basis for much more accurate and powerful interpretations relating to both the commonalities of trends and the actual effects of policies, practices, and other interventions within and across nations/militaries. We would hope, as well, that in those areas where incidents of harassment and/or discrimination continue to be regularly reported or observed, more effective preventive and enforcement mechanisms would be found in dealing with them.

NOTES

1   Catharine A. MacKinnon, *Sexual Harassment of Working Women*, Yale University Press, 1979.

2   The case studies include the 1995 Australia Defence Force (ADF) Sexual Harassment Study, the 2000 Survey of Experiences of Unacceptable Behaviour in the ADF, the 1992 Canadian Forces (CF) Personal Harassment Questionnaire, the 1998 CF Harassment Survey, the 1995 New Zealand Defence Force (NZDF) Survey of the Incidence and Management of Harassment, the 1995 United States Department of Defense (DoD) Sexual Harassment Study, the 1996 United States Armed Forces Equal Opportunity Survey, and 1989-2000 administrations of the United States Naval Equal Opportunity and Sexual Harassment (NEOSH) Survey.

3   Australia, Canada and New Zealand make reference to prohibited grounds of discrimination within their questionnaires. In Canada, for example, the prohibited grounds of discrimination are identified within the *Canadian Human Rights Act*.

4   A. L. Culbertson, P. Rosenfeld, and C. E. Newell, *Sexual Harassment in the Active Duty Navy: Findings from the 1991 Navy-wide Survey*, sed 92152-7250, TR-94-2 (San Diego, CA: Navy Personnel Research and Development Center, 1993).

5   For example, the U.S. Armed Forces Equal Opportunity Survey used "made you feel uncomfortable by hostile looks or stares because of your race/ethnicity" as a survey response item, and harassment surveys in Canada, New Zealand, and the United States used "sexually suggestive looks, gestures or body language".

6   For example, the United States Equal Opportunity Survey used "I was rated lower than I deserved on my last evaluation" as a survey response item, while the 1992 and 1998 Canadian Forces Harassment questionnaires included "unfairness in the evaluation of your job performance".

7   Michael Power, *A Survey of Experiences of Unacceptable Behaviour in the Australian Defence Force* (Canberra: Director Strategic Personnel Planning and Research, Defence Personnel Executive Program, Department of Defence, 2001). Power, *A Survey of Experiences of Unacceptable Behaviour in the Australian Defence Force.*

8   Jane E. Adams-Roy, *Harassment in the Canadian Forces: Results of the 1998 Survey*, Sponsor Research Report 99-11 (Director Human Resources Research and Evaluation, Department of National Defence, Canada, 1999).

9   Lisa Bastian, Anita Lancaster, and Heidi Reyst, *Department of Defense 1995 Sexual Harassment Survey*, DMDC Report No. 96-014 (Arlington, VA: Defense Manpower Data Center, 1996); R. O. Simmons, *Sexual Harassment Surveys of the U.S. and Australian Armed Forces*, Technical Panel HUM-TP3, Military Human Resources Issues, TTCP/HUM/98/006 (1998).

10   "The Sexual Experience Questionnaire" (SEQ) is considered a psychometrically sound measure of sexual harassment and has been used to measure sexual experience in several military organizations. See L. F. Fitzgerald, V. J. Magley, F. Drasgow, and C. R. Waldo, "Measuring Sexual Harassment in the Military: The Sexual Experiences Questionnaire (SEQ-DoD)," *Military Psychology* 11(3) (1999): 243-263.

11   Simmons, *Sexual Harassment Surveys.*

12   Ibid.

13   L.F. Fitzgerald, S. Shullman, N. Bailey, M. Richards, J. Swecker, A. Gold, A. J. Ormerod, and L. Weitzman, "The Incidence and Dimensions of Sexual Harassment in Academia and the Workplace," *Journal of Vocational Behavior* 32 (1988): 152-175.

14   K. Quinn, S*exual Harassment in the Australian Defence Force: A comparative assessment of results from the 1987 ADF Career and Family Study and the 1995 ADF Career and Family Study* (Canberra: Director Publishing and Visual Communications Defence Centre, 1996).

15   Unless otherwise indicated, observations in reference to changes in incident rates noted throughout this chapter are intended to convey general trends in respondent reporting/harassment incident rates rather than statistical significance. In most cases, data resulting from statistical tests of significance were not available.

16   Quinn, *Sexual Harassment in the Australian Defence Force.*

17   Power, *A Survey of Experiences of Unacceptable Behaviour in the Australian Defence Force.*

18   Ibid.

19   Ibid.

20   Ibid.

21   R. J. Hansen, *Personal Harassment in the Canadian Forces: 1992 Survey, Working Paper* 93-1 (Canadian Forces Personnel Applied Research Unit, Department of National Defence, 1993).

22   Adams-Roy, Harassment in the Canadian Forces. .

23   Ibid.

24   Good Working Review, *Report of the Review of Good Working Relationships in the New Zealand Defence Force* (New Zealand Defence Force, 1995).

25   Ibid.

26   Bastian et al., *Department of Defense 1995 Sexual Harassment Survey.*

27   Ibid.

28   Jacquelyn Scarville, Scott Button, Jack Edwards, Anita Lancaster, and Timothy Elig, *Armed Forces Equal Opportunity Survey*, DMDC Report No. 97-027 (Arlington, VA: Defense Manpower Data Center, 1999).

29   Ibid.

30   A. L. Culbertson, P. Rosenfeld, S. Booth-Kewley, and P. Magnusson, *Assessment of Sexual Harassment in the Navy: Results of the 1989 Navy-wide Survey*, 92152-6800, TR-92-11 (San Diego, CA: Navy Personnel Research and Development Center, 1992).

31   Ibid; Paul Rosenfeld, Carol Newell, and Sharon Le, "Equal Opportunity Climate of Women and Minorities in the Navy: Results from the Navy Equal Opportunity/Sexual Harassment (NEOSH) Survey," *Military Psychology* 10 (1998): 69-85.

32   Culbertson et al., *Assessment of Sexual Harassment in the Navy: Findings from the 1989 Navy-wide Survey.*

33   Culbertson et al., *Sexual Harassment in the Active Duty Navy: Findings from the 1991 Navy-wide Survey.*

34   Chief of Naval Operations, *Results of the 1999-2000 Navy Equal Opportunity Sexual Harassment (NEOSH) Survey* (GENADMIN/CNO WASHINGTON DC/N09 292211Z MAR 01, Administrative Message, 29 March 01).

35   Ibid.

36   One notable exception to this trend is an absolute increase from 2 to 3 per cent, between 1992 and 1998, among male Canadian Forces members reporting experience of sexual harassment. This increase was not reported as a statistically significant measure, and there is no evidence of this type of increase in the other case studies. However, as the demographic characteristics of military organizations become increasingly diverse, varying patterns of harassment and discrimination will provide valuable insights for leadership.

DEMOGRAPHICS AND DIVERSITY ISSUES IN CANADIAN MILITARY PARTICIPATION[1]

CHRISTIAN LEUPRECHT

INTRODUCTION

Throughout the world's liberal democracies, changing labour market characteristics are affecting human resource acquisition in an all-volunteer military. This is especially the case in nations such as Australia, the United States, and Canada, where the large, aging "baby-boom generation"[2] is about to disappear from the active labour force—the military included. This is coupled with vast increases in ethno-cultural and other forms of social differentiation and diversification in recruitment markets. As the country with the lowest fertility rate among traditional immigrant-settler countries[3], Canada is finding the recruitment and retention of women, visible minorities, and Aboriginals to the Canadian Forces (CF) an increasingly important concern.

Policies of multiculturalism are now found throughout Western countries, but Canada is the world's only sovereign federation that formally recognizes a national minority, ethnic minorities, and Aboriginal peoples. Unlike other liberal democracies, Canada's official multiculturalism and related policies enshrine diversity and associated operational practices both in its legal statutes and in its Constitution.[4] The term "national minority" refers to groups that were present when the state was founded; Canada is generally understood to have one national minority: francophones. "Ethnic minorities" refers to identifiable immigrant groups that arrived after the state was founded; "Aboriginal people" were those present when the state was founded but, at the time, were not acknowledged as equal stakeholders in the political process. This taxonomy follows a line of now well-established research on groups showing that the conditions they face and the claims they advance, differ according to these three categories. Furthermore, for the purpose of this chapter, the term "ethnic minorities" refers to visible minorities (as opposed to linguistic or Aboriginal minorities).[5] This understanding conforms to that of Canada's employment equity legislation, which defines as a minority those persons, other than Aboriginals, who are not of Caucasian ancestry or whose phenotype is not white-skinned. The distinction between francophones and visible minorities is not totally watertight, since a sizable proportion of French-speaking persons also self-identify as visible minorities.

Canada's multiculturalism policy has created a wide range of ethnic organizations, including youth groups, that have been co-opted into the state,[6] and Canada enjoys better relations with communities of recent immigrants than do many other democracies.[7] Still, attracting women, visible minorities, and Aboriginals (including women and "status Indians" in the latter) has been fraught with difficulty.

After conducting a 1997 Public Opinion Survey of qualifications and interest in military service among Canada's prime recruitment market (i.e., the 17 to 29 years of age cohort), the CF adopted the following representational percentages as recruiting objectives in 1999: 3 percent Aboriginals, 9 percent visible minorities and 28 percent women.[8] Although the magnitude of the challenge has been shrinking, with the possible exception of Aboriginals (whose representation is skewed by their predominance among Canadian Rangers) the CF still falls short of these targets, especially in the Regular Force.[9]

The pool of interested female and francophone recruits is shrinking while that of visible minorities and Aboriginals is growing. Since recruitment and retention patterns are inextricably linked, the failure to optimize recruitment potential across all target groups is likely to perpetuate overall instability in human-resource management and will also drive up costs over time. In order to improve this situation, the CF recently implemented a four-year recruitment and retention strategy.[10]

This chapter argues that the strategy's long-term viability hinges on greater ethno-cultural diversity in the CF. The first section provides a cursory survey of intervening variables and current policies. Subsequent sections contrast the representation of women and minorities in Canadian society with that in the CF. The findings suggest that a focus on the traditional pool of francophones and women alone is unlikely to solve the CF's recruitment difficulties – especially in the longer term and under favourable economic conditions. Thus, in order to take advantage of their growing demographic weight in the Canadian population *and* in the potential recruitment pool, attention needs to be paid to minorities.

BACKGROUND

In countries with volunteer militaries, such as Canada, the opportunity cost associated with recruitment is a function of the size of the recruitable cohort which, in turn, is influenced by such intervening variables as the economy and attitudes towards the military. In general, opportunity cost increases as the Force expands. The larger the size of the Force, the more difficult, and thus the more costly, it is to recruit the requisite quantity and quality of talent.[11] Recruitment is heavily influenced by economic conditions and labour-force dynamics, which include social and employment preferences.[12] Canada's tightening labour market and the impending wave of retiring CF baby boomers does not bode well for recruitment and retention.[13] It is easier for the CF to recruit during macro-economic downturns and in geographic areas with high chronic unemployment levels than it is in times of high economic growth and in areas where unemployment levels are low.[14] Also, generally speaking, the lengthened time spent on education keeps young people, especially the "best and brightest", out of the recruitment pool. Third, the decline in the number of veterans – which is more a function of leaner militaries than of fewer conflicts – means there are fewer direct sources of encouragement for young people to join the military. [15]

During the 1980s, following the promulgation of the *Canadian Human Rights Act* and the *Charter of Rights and Freedoms*, the CF removed restrictive age eligibility requirements for entry, thus permitting older Canadians to apply for military service. With the exception of the combat arms, some seafaring occupations, and jet fighter pilots, age has become less significant for recruitment; but for a variety of reasons, the most desirable segment of the older population (i.e., 25 years and above) is difficult to recruit. First, many older prospective recruits already hold other gainful employment.[16] Second, older recruits are more likely to have a working spouse and children, which makes the nomadic lifestyle of a military career more problematic for them. Third, private-sector compensation tends to show greater sensitivity to rapidly changing labour market conditions than does the public sector, and this often makes the latter less competitive in the active labour market. Increased employment opportunities tend to exert rapid upward pressure on wages, the adjustment to which the military finds difficult. Thus as real and projected labour shortages drive up wages, the military is placed in a position of diminishing returns in its quest for qualified candidates.[17] The overall effect of the above conditions, along with other unique features and demands of the military, may well make it appear less attractive to older, well-qualified labour-force participants, regardless of their ethno-cultural affiliation.

This chapter examines issues pertinent to three conceptually-distinct types of diversity – gender, linguistic, and ethno-cultural— which form a significant part of the CF's human resource management pool. Women are not a minority in the strictest sense, as they constitute about half the population at any given time. By contrast, linguistic and ethno-cultural diversity is usually associated with those groups that do not enjoy a plurality among the population.

Empirical evidence from an internal self-identification census (with admitted methodological flaws) lends some support for the distinctness of women in relation to minorities, based on their assessed CF employment barriers.[18] While women and minorities identify a number of common barriers, they also perceive somewhat different challenges within the CF. Among other barriers, women are particularly concerned about promotion prospects, whereas visible minorities alone perceive the lack of knowledge of cultural diversity and the lack of cultural accommodation by the CF and its members. While analysts indicate that attrition is of concern for both groups, perspectives on the subject differ among them.[19]

An analysis of the results of the CF Diversity Survey, undertaken in 1995, found that the low level of representation for women is the result of under-recruitment and a substantially higher rate of attrition than that of men. Results of the analysis also showed that average rates of promotion were lower for women than for men in the senior officer and senior non-commissioned member (NCM) ranks.[20] To mitigate these gender effects (see below), the CF implemented an Employment Equity (EE) Plan, which distinguishes between "employment equity" and "gender integration". Gender integration is defined in terms of outcome. For example, in *Brown v. Canadian Armed Forces*, the Canadian Human Rights Tribunal ordered that all obstacles to the integration of women into the military to be removed and *that full integration be achieved by 1999*".[21] Employment equity, by contrast, is a non-discrimination formula, designed to remove barriers: most specifically, to "achieve equality in the workplace so that no person shall be denied employment opportunities or benefits for reasons unrelated to ability and, in the fulfillment of that goal, to correct the disadvantageous employment conditions experienced by women, Aboriginal peoples, persons with disabilities and members of visible minorities" (*Employment Equity Act of Canada, Section 2*). That is, employment equity is concerned solely with equality of condition, not with outcome: "The statutory obligations of the Act require the CF to search out any adverse effects or systemic discrimination created by its practices and policies and, if any are found, to determine their cause and make changes".[22] Whether or not the removal of barriers actually precipitates greater participation by Designated Group Members (DGMs) is immaterial to the non-discrimination approach. Yet outcome is, of course, indicative of condition, so non-discrimination is not to be confounded with multiculturalism. A policy is, by definition, not multicultural in nature unless it is expressly designed to enhance ethno-cultural participation.

The following sections deal with issues related to the potential (from societal statistics) and actual (from CF statistics) representation of women, francophones, visible minorities, and Aboriginals in the CF, using data that show actual (historical and current) population distributions, as well as future projections.

WOMEN

The Canadian population's relatively stable gender/sex ratio notwithstanding, Figure 1 shows that there has been enough of a change that women are now in the majority.

By late 2003, women comprised 16.3 percent of the entire CF. However, this reflects female recruitment into the Reserve Force, which has had greater success at attracting women than has the Regular Force. The aggregate increase of 19.4 percent between 1997 and 2002 is thus deceiving. The Regular Force proportion grew by

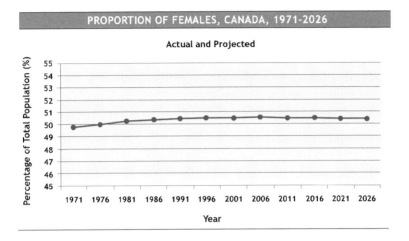

FIGURE 1.   PROPORTION OF FEMALES, CANADA, 1971-2026

(SOURCE: M.V. GEORGE, SHIRLEY LOH, RAVI B.P. VERMA, AND Y. EDWARD SHIN. POPULATION PROJECTIONS FOR CANADA, PROVINCES AND TERRITORIES, 2001-2026 (OTTAWA: STATISTICS CANADA, 2001). 91-520-XPB.)

13.9 percent between 1997 and 2002, compared to 22 percent for the Reserve.[23] While women in the reserves are approaching the 23 percent mark, their proportion in the regulars appears to have reached a plateau at around 12 percent. Compared to the ceiling of 1,500 women in 1971, the current membership of 7,100 women represents an increase of about 375 percent. Despite these inroads into the representation of women, the overall CF still falls 42 percent short, and the Regular Force falls 55 percent short, of the latent potential identified by the 1997 Public Opinion Survey.

FRANCOPHONES

As Figure 2 shows, in 2002, the proportion of francophones among the Canadian population reached a historical nadir of 22.9 percent. That contrasts with a francophone rate of participation in the CF of 27.4 percent in 2004. Whereas the proportion of francophones in the population continues to decline, the ratio of francophones to

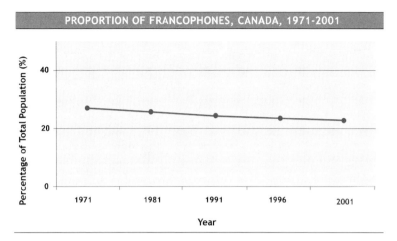

FIGURE 2. PROPORTION OF FRANCOPHONES, CANADA, 1971-2001
(SOURCE: GEORGE ET AL., OP. CIT., 2001.)

anglophones in the CF has changed little in recent years. Nonetheless, during the 1990s, the proportion of francophones in the senior ranks actually doubled.[24] However, given that the CF excels in the recruitment of the country's national minority while visible minorities, Aboriginals and women get short shrift suggests that success in recruiting minorities may be more a function of internal CF policies and practices than of sociological or other external constraints.

VISIBLE MINORITIES

Between 1986 and 2001, the proportion of Canada's visible minority population doubled, to 13.4 percent (Figure 3). By 2003, about 4.2 percent of the CF regular members identified themselves as visible minorities; thus the CF's visible-minority population doubled over the course of five years. Still, that level falls more than 50 percent short of the latent potential identified in the 1997 Public Opinion Survey.

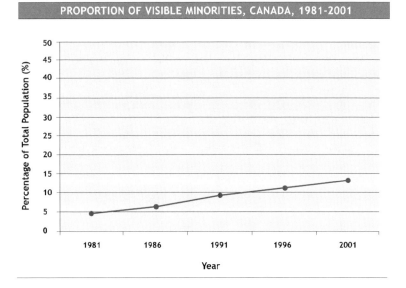

FIGURE 3.   PROPORTION   OF   VISIBLE-MINORITY   POPULATION,
CANADA, 1981-2001

(SOURCE: CANADA'S ETHNOCULTURAL PORTRAIT: THE CHANGING MOSAIC (OTTAWA:
STATISTICS CANADA, ANALYSIS SERIES, 2003)

ABORIGINAL CANADIANS

Aboriginals are the fastest-growing component of the Canadian population (Figure 4) and, by definition, should realistically form an increasing proportion of the CF's recruiting potential. Eighty percent are under the age of 30 .

Yet, Aboriginals constitute only 2.3 percent of the Regular Force.[25] That is still about 50 percent higher than the 1.5 percent who so identified themselves in 1997. The growth, however, has been almost exclusively among Non-Status Indians.[26] Furthermore, and in stark contrast to visible minorities and women, Table 1 shows that Aboriginal representation in the the non-commissioned ranks

Population

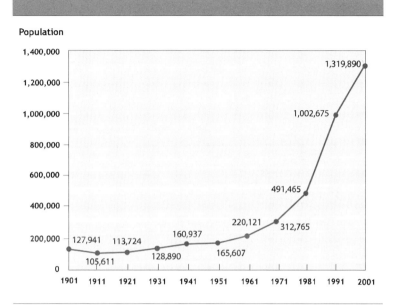

FIGURE 4. POPULATION REPORTING ABORIGINAL ORIGIN, CANADA, 1901 - 2001

(SOURCE: ABORIGINAL PEOPLES OF CANADA: A DEMOGRAPHIC PROFILE (OTTAWA: STATISTICS CANADA, ANALYSIS SERIES, 2003)

exceeds their representation in the commissioned ranks. In short, the CF has difficulty recruiting among Status Indians, attracting Aboriginals to the officer corps, and in retaining Aboriginals. From the figures it follows that the Canadian Forces Recruitment Group is meeting its annual targets. Problems of accessibility, mobility, retention, and equality of opportunity, by contrast, persist.

On the positive side, progress in Aboriginal recruitment outpaces Aboriginal increases in the actual population.[27] Moreover, the latent potential identified in the 1997 Survey has been captured and even exceeded. But, as one recruiter's guide notes, "[i]f Aboriginals participated in proportion to their representation in the country's population, there would be about 3,700 members, or two-and-one-half times the number presently reported."[28]

DESIGNATED GROUP	NCMS	OFFICERS
Women	10.7%	23.3%
Aboriginal Peoples	3.3%	1.6%
Visible Minorities	3.6%	4.3%

TABLE 1. TOTAL REPRESENTATION OF NON-COMMISSION MEMBERS AND OFFICERS BY DESIGNATED GROUP FOR THE TOTAL CANADIAN FORCES

(SOURCE: NICOLA J. HOLDEN, THE CANADIAN FORCES 2001 SELF-IDENTIFICATION CENSUS: METHODOLOGY AND PRELIMINARY RESULT, DEPARTMENT OF NATIONAL DEFENCE, DIRECTOR OF STRATEGIC HUMAN RESOURCES, RESEARCH NOTE 01/2003, P. 8)

DISCUSSION

The CF excels in its recruitment of women, even though, owing to their higher turnover rates in the past, their proportion of the CF population has remained fairly static. Concomitantly, the CF over-recruits in ever-increasing proportions among francophones, in relation to their representation in the Canadian population. At the same time, the CF has made only limited inroads among the second-fastest growing component of the Canadian population, visible minorities. Even so, relative to their rate of growth among the Canadian population, the CF fares better among visible minorities than it does among Aboriginals. The latter are being recruited less successfully than women, francophones, and visible minorities even though the Aboriginal Canadian population is growing faster than any of those groups. Moreover, the rate of participation among visible minorities and Aboriginals is unrepresentative relative to their population size and potential.

Employment equity is claimed to be "about maintaining and enhancing operational effectiveness".[29] Ergo, the extent to which efficiency in drawing from the total recruitable population enters into such an "effectiveness matrix", the above suggests the CF is not maintaining, let alone enhancing, operational effectiveness. To the contrary, these observations suggest the CF is falling further behind. The issue has been put by CF human-resource policy itself in practical or empirical terms, as the following quote from the CF's EE Plan indicates: "In the year 2000, 80% of people entering the workforce will be designated group members [DGMs]. If CF policies and practices do not encourage DGMs to enroll, the CF will face a shrinking labour pool from which to seek the best and most qualified recruits"[30] In other words, the issue of recruitment across the various DGM groups is primarily practical rather than ethical.

These observations point to a hastening problem. In 1950, 92 percent of Canada's population growth was a function of natural increase. At the height of the baby boom, in 1959, the fertility rate averaged 3.9 children (live births) per woman. By 1972, however, fertility levels had dropped below replacement levels. Fertility currently registers at 1.6 children per woman and is projected to drop to 1.2 during the next two decades.[31] To maintain its current population size, Canada will have to take in an estimated 260,000 immigrants per year with the result that, by 2050, over half the country's population will have been born abroad.

Irrespective of its political likelihood, immigration of such magnitude is sociologically feasible. Research carried out over the past 20 years has replaced economic push-pull theories of migration with "kin networks" based on political geography: People are most likely to move where they already have a kin network.[32] Kin networks figure prominently in countries such as Canada where a diaspora of various ethnic and visible minorities already has a critical mass (Figure 5).

In effect, among liberal democracies, Canada is already second only to Australia in the proportion of its foreign-born population, as demonstrated by Figure 6.

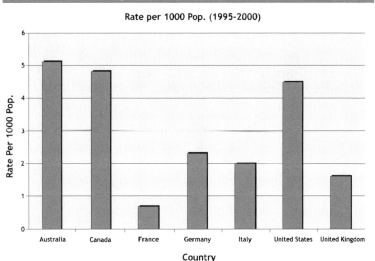

FIGURE 5.   NET MIGRATION (ANNUAL AVERAGE) - RATE PER 1,000
           POP., CANADA, 1995-2000

(SOURCE: UN INTERNATIONAL MIGRATION REPORT, 2002)

Notwithstanding its relatively small population size, compared to other liberal democracies, Canada ranks fourth in terms of its foreign-born population (after the U.S., Germany, and France). In fact, over half of Canada's net population growth is the result of immigration. Most immigrants are not only visible minorities, but, as Table 2 shows, they come increasingly from Asia and the Middle East.

While socio-fragmentation is on the rise in Canadian society, the analysis of recruitment patterns suggests that the CF has not been capitalizing on this trend to the extent that it could. However, now that it is CF military doctrine to venture beyond mere representation and instead work actively towards harnessing the values and benefits of an integrated fighting force one would anticipate a concerted effort to that end.[33] Figure 7 depicts the degree to which the

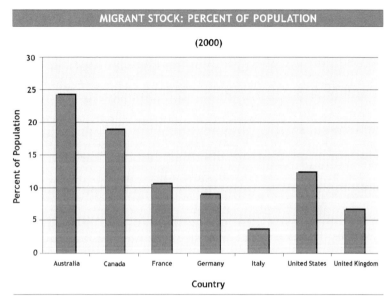

FIGURE 6. MIGRANT STOCK - PERCENT OF POPULATION, 2000

(SOURCE: UNITED NATIONS. INTERNATIONAL MIGRATION REPORT, 2002)

proportion of Caucasians and francophones is on the wane, and the proportion of visible minorities is on the rise.

The CF projects that by 2011 below-replacement rates of fertility and allophone immigration–immigrants who employ neither official language (English or French) as their vernacular–will have reduced francophones to 14 percent of the Canadian population and anglophones to 47 percent, with the remaining 39 percent of the population comprising people who do not identify as anglophone, francophone, or Canadian. That is more than double the 2001 population, when the combined proportion of this population approached 18 percent of the Canadian population. The decline in official bi-linguistic and bi-cultural diversity is offset by a rise in multi-cultural diversity. Should current recruitment patterns persist, the CF's composition will diverge

COUNTRY	2000			2001			2002		
	NUM.	%	RANK	NUM.	%	RANK	NUM.	%	RANK
China, People's Republic of	36,716	16.15	1	40,315	16.09	1	33,231	14.51	1
India	26,088	11.48	2	27,848	11.12	2	28,815	12.58	2
Pakistan	14,184	6.24	3	15,341	6.12	3	14,164	6.18	3
Philippines	10,088	4.44	4	12,914	5.16	4	11,000	4.80	4
Iran	5,608	2.47	8	5,737	2.29	7	7,742	3.38	5
Korea, Republic of	7,629	3.35	5	9,604	3.83	5	7,326	3.20	6
Romania	4,425	1.95	11	5,585	2.23	8	5,692	2.48	7
United States	5,815	2.56	7	5,902	2.36	6	5,288	2.31	8
Sri Lanka	5,841	2.57	6	5,514	2.20	9	4,961	2.17	9
United Kingdom	4,647	2.04	10	5,350	2.14	10	4,720	2.06	10
Yugoslavia	4,723	2.08	9	2,788	1.11	22	1,620	0.71	31
Total for Top Ten Only	121,339	53.39	-	134,110	53.54	-	122,939	53.67	-
Total Other Countries	106,007	46.61	-	116,374	46.46	-	106,152	46.33	-
TOTAL	227,346	100	-	250,484	100	-	229,091	100	-

TABLE 2. LEADING COUNTRIES OF IMMIGRATION, CANADA, 2000-2002

(SOURCE: CITIZENSHIP AND IMMIGRATION CANADA, 2002; SEE ALSO RAVI PENDAKUR AND JENNA HENNEBRY. *MULTICULTURALISM CANADA: A DEMOGRAPHIC OVERVIEW* (OTTAWA: DEPARTMENT OF CANADIAN HERITAGE, STRATEGIC RESEARCH AND BUSINESS PLANNING MULTICULTURALISM, 1998))

increasingly from the ethno-demographic composition of Canadian society.

An interesting wrinkle may be inferred from this socio-demographic analysis: The sustainability of a bilingual military goes hand in hand with a more multi-cultural military. With the proportion of francophones on the wane due to low fertility, the fastest-growing French-speaking population is found among visible minorities. Far from being mutually exclusive, the CF's bilingualist and multiculturalist mandates are thus complementary.

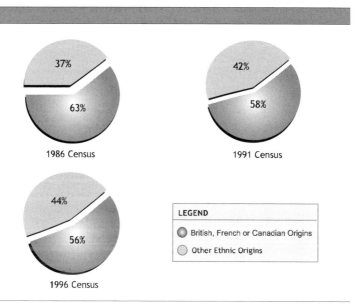

FIGURE 7:   POPULATION REPORTING AT LEAST ONE ETHNIC ORIGIN
             OTHER THAN BRITISH, FRENCH OR CANADIAN, 1986,
             1991 AND 1996 CENSUSES

(SOURCE: A GRAPHIC OVERVIEW OF DIVERSITY IN CANADA (OTTAWA: DEPARTMENT OF
CANADIAN HERITAGE, STRATEGIC RESEARCH - MULTICULTURALISM 2 AUGUST 2000)

The glacial pace at which DGMs are finding their way into the
military, let alone into the senior ranks, leads to less than optimal
human resource outcomes, certainly from a representational
perspective. Of this, the CF is fully cognizant.[34] Moreover, this
situation has long been projected by Canadian socio-demographic
researchers.[35] However, the juxtaposition of current recruitment
patterns, relative to the projected ethno-cultural fragmentation of
the Canadian population, bespeaks a more serious concern than was
the case in the past.

The CF's own projections (see Figure 8 below) show a shrinking
recruitable age (15 to 29) cohort as a proportion of the population.

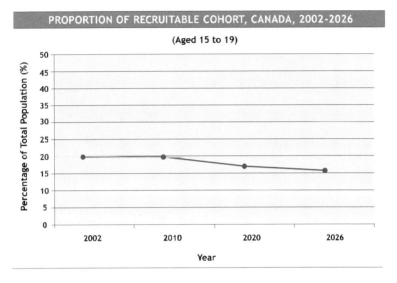

(Aged 15 to 19)

FIGURE 8: PROPORTION OF RECRUITABLE COHORT (AGE 15 TO 29), CANADA, 2002-26

(SOURCE: MILITARY HR STRATEGY 2020: *FACING THE PEOPLE OF THE FUTURE* (OTTAWA: MINISTER OF NATIONAL DEFENCE, 2002) D2-139-2002, P. 19.)

The size of the Caucasian population and the potential recruit population are shrinking. If over-reliance on this traditional pool of recruits persists, the CF's human recourse will be increasingly strained,. There are at least two promising trends. Both, however, could prove problematic. First, the number and proportion of women are on the rise, and second, the proportion of Aboriginals is also increasing. We need to examine these more closely. The pool of potential recruits from the Caucasian female population is becoming shallower; therefore, greater success in recruiting and retaining women is a tenuous solution if substantial numbers of women are not also drawn from minority groups.[36] The total recruitable cohort of women between the ages of 15 and 29 is starting to shrink. At the same time, the potential recruit population of visible minorities is expanding, owing to larger

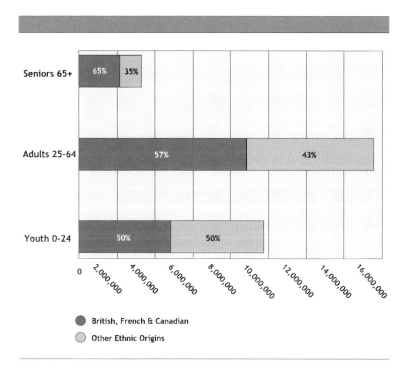

FIGURE 9: AGE COHORTS BY BROAD ETHNIC GROUPS, CANADA, 1996

(SOURCE: A GRAPHIC OVERVIEW OF DIVERSITY IN CANADA (OTTAWA: DEPARTMENT OF
CANADIAN HERITAGE, STRATEGIC RESEARCH - MULTICULTURALISM 2 AUGUST 2000))

family sizes among recent immigrants. The youngest age-cohorts
(0-24) are the most diverse. Figure 9 shows that half of all Canadian
children currently have at least one ethnic origin affiliation other
than British, French, Canadian or Aboriginal.

In 1999, 13 percent of the population in the under-25 age-cohort had
a visible-minority background and 7 percent were of Aboriginal
descent.[37] Although immigrants accounted for only 13.4 percent of
Canada's population in 2001, they comprised 19.9 percent of the
labour force. What is more, almost 70 percent of growth in the
Canadian workforce has been due to recent immigrants.

In 2000, Aboriginals made up 10 percent and visible minorities 9 percent of the recruitable population cohorts.[38] By 2011, immigration is projected to account for virtually all labour-force growth. By 2016, 24 percent of the recruitable cohort – or 1 million of a cohort of 3.5 million   – will be comprised of visible minorities.[39] It follows that the recruitable cohort of visible minority women must also be expanding. Giving priority to ethno-cultural diversity over gender diversity is thus likely to produce better human-resource outcomes in the long run. Since this is a counter-factual hypothesis, one cannot be certain that it would actually obtain such. But with the total recruitable cohort of women in Canadian society on the wane, a reversal of the CF's present strategy – giving priority to the recruitment of minorities over women – may very well improve human-resource outcomes because it would direct attention toward a growing, rather than stagnant, latent recruit population.

The data provides some support for this claim. Since Aboriginals constitute a rapidly growing component of the Canadian population, the greater the emphasis on the minority population, the more women the CF is likely to be able to attract. Despite their relatively rapid growth in absolute terms, the Aboriginal population remains small relative to Canada's burgeoning foreign-born population. Currently, Canada counts 1.4 million Aboriginals relative to a foreign-born population of 5.5 million and a visible minority population of 4.2 million. Since growth among Canada's Aboriginal population is exclusively a function of natural increase whereas growth among the visible minority population is a function of natural increase and migration, the gap between the proportion of the Aboriginal population and the proportion of the visible-minority population is narrowing.

However, the size of families among recent immigrants statistically exceeds the Canadian norm. As a result, the gap is not narrowing at a sufficiently rapid rate to justify giving priority to Aboriginals over minorities. Between 1991 and 2001, for instance, Canada's visible minority population increased by about two thirds. That compares to a rate of growth of 32 percent for Canada's Aboriginal population over the same period. In other words, Canada's Aboriginals have a younger population structure than its visible minorities do, but the proportion of visible minorities among the Canadian population is growing more rapidly than that of Aboriginals.

Ergo, despite the positive correlation between the recruitment of women and the recruitment of Aboriginals, the orders of magnitude do not warrant a substantial reallocation of resources to that effect. To be sure, more needs to be learned about why some groups, such as non-status Indians, are more predisposed to joining the military than other groups, such as Status Indians; why some groups are more attracted to some branches and trades of the military than are other groups; why there are different rates of attrition for different groups, and so forth.

CONCLUSION AND IMPLICATIONS

The military decision-maker, at least in Canada, faces a dilemma: Should the CF reflect the composition of Canadian society or should it seek to fill its overall recruitment target at the lowest cost? The prevailing wisdom on recruitment holds that ethical and pratical economics considerations are incompatible. However, the analysis in this chapter reframes them as components in a "positive-sum" game. In light of Canada's changing ethnic composition, there are only two policy options to attain the required military participation rates: to recruit more diversely, or to recruit more intensively among groups that are in decline.

Cameron Ross, for instance, is a proponent of the latter strategy;[40] but both the demographic evidence and the CF's EE Plan, along with its supporting documentation, suggest the need for a more comprehensive approach. The first view is that the CF would meet its recruitment targets more readily and more cost-effectively if, instead of "social engineering", it focused on its traditional area of recruiting strength, i.e., Caucasian rural Canada. This proposition is not persuasive; 80 percent of Canadians – and an even larger proportion of the recruitable age cohorts – reside in urban areas. More generally, the pool of Caucasian recruits has become increasingly shallow. While it may be cheaper to recruit at the margins for a time, eventually this approach will be self-defeating, from the standpoints of quantity, quality and cost. Broad ethno-cultural recruitment may initially be a slow and costly process, the efforts should prove more productive in the end.

A "zero-sum game" mentality that sets up an opposition between the ethics of recruitment and the economics of recruitment, in which one must be chosen over the other, is likely to be unproductive in the longer term. In fact, a socio-demographic approach to CF recruitment – as follows from the trends presented in this chapter – one that gives weight to representational issues (the ethics of recruitment) but which focuses heavily on the areas of greatest recruiting potential (practical efficiency) – is likely to be both the most fiscally sound and most ethically defensible alternative in a diverse, liberal-democratic society. Nor should the focus be on ethno-cultural groups in general only, since virtually one-half of those populations are women who, research suggests, will need special attention from the military, both from the point of view of understanding the barriers they perceive to their full participation, and in ways in which such barriers may be overcome. This is central to the development of a strategic human-resource management approach that encompasses and accommodates diversity.

NOTES

1   Nicolette O'Connor and Alex Dissette provided research assistance for this paper. The author also thanks the Social Sciences and Humanities Research Council of Canada for its continued support.

2   For a comprehensive description and discussion of the "baby boomers" – persons born from roughly 1946 to 1962 – and their impact on the labour force and other segments of society, as well as on subsequent generations, see David K. Foot (with Daniel Stoffman). *Boom, Bust and Echo* (Toronto: Macfarlane, Walter & Ross, 1996). Australia, Canada, and the United States have the most distinct "baby boom" generation-effect of any of the liberal democratic countries, primarily owing to massive increases in birthrates that began immediately after the end of the Second World War.

3   United Nations, *World Fertility Report 2003.*

4   See Will Kymlicka, "Being Canadian," *Government and Opposition* 38(3) 2003: 374-375 and "Canadian Multiculturalism in Historical and Comparative Perspective: Is Canada Unique?" *Constitutional Forum* 13(1) 2003: 1-8.

5   Will Kymlicka, *Multicultural Citizenship* (Oxford: Oxford University Press, 1995.

6   *Multiculturalism: The Evidence Series.* Vol 3: Multiculturalism Promotes Integration and Citizenship (Ottawa: Public Works and Government Services, 1998). See also Will Kymlicka, "Citizenship and Identity in Canada" in *Canadian Politics: Third Edition*, eds. Alain-G. Gagnon and James Bickerton (Broadview Press, 1999), pp. 19-38 and *Finding Our Way* (Don Mills, ON: Oxford University Press, 1995), chapter 1.

7   Andrew Parkin and Matthew Mendelsohn, *A New Canada: An Identity Shaped by Diversity* (Montreal: Centre for Research and Information on Canada, 2003). By contrast, the events at Kane(h)satake during the Oka crisis continue to strain the relationship between Aboriginals and the Canadian state. As a matter of fact, a CF recruitment guide explicitly instructs recruiters to "[a]void the following references: the conflict at Oka, Quebec [and] the dispute at Ipperwash, Ontario. …The 1990 incident is still an emotional topic with many First Nations. It invokes negative images of the CF and any reference to Oka should be avoided in a First Nations setting" [Harvey McCue, Strengthening Relationships *Between the Canadian Forces and Aboriginal People* (National Defence, Ottawa: 1999)].

8   *Survey of Visible Minorities, Aboriginals and Women To Assess Their Level of Interest in Joining The Canadian Forces* (A) (Toronto: Environics Research Group Limited, June 1997).

9   *Report of the Minister's Advisory Board for Gender Integration and Employment Equity* (MABGIEE) (Ottawa: Government of Canada Printing, March 2001); Nicola J. Holden, *The Canadian Forces 2001 Self-Identification Census: Methodology and Preliminary Result*, Department of National Defence, Director of Strategic Human Resources, research note 01/2003, p. 10. For a variety of reasons, including the highly subjective nature of self-identification and response error, results tend to be inaccurate.

10   See, for example, Franklin C. Pinch, *Selected Issues and Constraints on Full Gender Integration in Elite Ground Combat Units in Canada* (Kingston, ON: FCP Human Resources Consulting, 2002).

11   That is, the costs of meeting the quantitative and qualitative recruitment targets rise

incrementally with the size of the Force. See Charles Cotton, and Franklin C. Pinch, "The Winds of Change" in *Life in the Rank and File*, eds. David R. Segal and Wallace H. Sinaiko (Washington: Pergamon-Brassey's International Defense Publishers, 1985).

12   Sy Sohn, "Random Effects Meta Analysis of Military Recruiting," *Omega* 24(2) April 1996: 141-151.

13   Jeff Tasseron, "Military Manning and the Revolution in Social Affairs," *Canadian Military Journal* 2(3) 2001: 54, 56; *Canadian Forces Recruitment Improvement Study* (National Defence, Ottawa: 2000), i; Victoria Edwards, "Don't Mention it! The Oka Crisis and the Recruitment of Aboriginal Peoples." Working paper presented in 2002 at the Canadian Defence Academy's 5th Annual Graduate Student Symposium in Kingston.

14   Since unemployment on reserves is about 60 percent, one might actually expect Aboriginals, and status Indians in particular (since they are concentrated on reserves) to be overrepresented in the CF (see McCue, *Strengthening Relationships*, 27). Since that is not the case, the observation suggests that other factors, such as culture and history, must factor into the decision whether to join the armed services.

15   Deborah Payne and John Warner, "The Military Recruiting Productivity Slowdown: The Roles of Resources, Opportunity Cost and the Tastes of Youth," *Defence and Peace Economics* 14(5) 2004: 329-342.

16   See, for example, Franklin C. Pinch, Claude Hamel, and Richard MacLennan. *What Do they Prefer?* Report Submitted to the Director of Military Employment Policy, National Defence Headquarters (Ottawa: HDP Incorporated, 2000) for a discussion of the difficulties surrounding skilled adult recruitment.

17   Robert P. Steel, "Labor Market Dimensions as Predictors of the Reenlistment Decisions of Military Personnel," *Journal of Applied Psychology* 81(4) April 1996: 421-428.

18   Employment Equity Plan (EE Plan): Building Teamwork in a Diverse Canadian Forces (Ottawa: Canadian Forces, 1999) 5320-28-15(DMGIEE), p. 9

19   Donna Winslow and Jason Dunn, "Women in the Canadian Forces: Between Legal and Social Integration," *Current Sociology* 50(5) 2002: 641-647. See also Leesa M. Tanner, *Gender integration in the Canadian Force: A quantitative and qualitative analysis* (Ottawa: Department of National Defence, Operational Research Division, Director General Operational Research, Directorate of Operational Research [Corporate, Air & Maritime; Director General Military Human Resources Policy & Planning, Director of Military Gender Integration & Employment Equity], 1999). On the link between attrition and female identity in the CF, see Karen D. Davis, "Understanding Women's Exit from the Canadian Forces" in *Warriors and Wives: Women and the Military in the United States and Canada*, eds. Laurie Weinstein ed and Christie C. White (Westport, Connecticut: Bergin & Garvey, 1997), 179-198 and Karen D. Davis, *Chief Land Staff Gender Integration Study: The Experience of Women Who Have Served in the Combat Arms*, Sponsor Research Report 98-1 (Ottawa, Canada: Personnel Research Team, National Defence, 1998). On gendered equipment see Nina Richman-Loo and Rachel Weber. "Gender and Weapon Design" in I*t's Our Military Too: Women and the US Army*, ed. Judith Hicks Stiehm (Philadelphia: Temple University, 1996), 136-155.

20   CF EE Plan, op. cit., 1999, p. 10.

21   Canadian Human Rights Tribunal. *Brown v. Canadian Armed Forces*. T.D. 3/1989. Emphasis added.

22   *Idem.*

23   *Ibid*, p. 10.

24   This is partly the result of the government-mandated requirement for English and French bilingualism among senior leaders in the CF -- a bilingual military was one of the recommendations of the Royal Commission on Bilingualism and Biculturalism -- and the fact that francophones are more likely than anglophones to have achieved bilingual status.

25   CF EE Plan, op. cit., 1999, p. 10.

26   A "Non-Status Indian" refers to a person of Indian ancestry who is not registered as an Indian in the Indian Register. Many of these individuals were simply not enrolled on treaty or band lists at the time enrolment was occurring, or were removed from the Registry due to enfranchisement provisions in the Indian Act.

27   *Registered Indian Population Projections for Canada and the Regions 2000-2021.* Total Registered Aboriginals (Ottawa: Indian and Northern Affairs Canada, 2000).

28   That level, incidentally, has actually been exceeded in the past. Aboriginal communities and Aboriginal families have a tradition of military service. Despite the total Aboriginal population being substantially smaller then than it is now and despite their exemption from conscription (since they were not yet legal Canadian citizens), proportionally they enlisted in numbers higher than any other segment of the Canadian population: 4,000 Aboriginal peoples joined the Canadian Expeditionary Force during World War I, while 6,000 enlisted during World War II (McCue, *Strengthening Relationships*, 28-29).

29   EE Plan 1999, p. 9

30   *Ibid*.

31   Tina Chui. "Canada's population charting into the 21st century," *Canadian Social Trends* 42 (Autumn 1996): 3–7.

32   Alejandro Portes and Robert L. Bach, *Latin Journal: Cuban and Mexican Immigrants in the United States* (Berkeley: University of California Press, 1985). See also Will Kymlicka. "Immigration, Citizenship, Multiculturalism: Exploring the Links" in *The Politics of Migration: Managing Opportunity, Conflict and Change*, ed. Sarah Spencer (Blackwell, Oxford, 2003), 195-208.

33   *Duty with Honour: The Profession of Arms in Canada* (Kingston, Ontario: Canadian Defence Academy – Canadian Forces Leadership Institute, 2003).

34   *Beyond Gender Integration Building Diversity in the CF* (Ottawa: Canadian Forces Employment Equity Plan, December 20, 1999); Delta Partners, op. cit., p. iv.

35   *The Military in a Changing Society: The Impact of Demographics on the CF* (Ottawa: National Defence, June 1997).

36   This finding reinforces the inaugural observations by Davis, *op. cit*, 2001.

37   Fernando Mata and John Valentine, *Selected Ethnic Profiles of Canada's Young Age Cohorts* (Ottawa: Department of Canadian Heritage, Citizens' Participation and Multiculturalism, Multiculturalism Program, Strategic Research and Analysis, 16 November 1999).

38   McCue, *Strengthening Relationships*, 28.

39   Tasseron, "Military Manning and the Revolution in Social Affairs,"w 56.

40   Cameron Ross, "Bled White and Bone Weary," BMSS thesis (Kingston: Royal Military College of Canada: 2000).

ORGANIZATIONAL VALUES AND CULTURAL DIVERSITY IN THE CANADIAN FORCES: THE CASE OF ABORIGINAL PEOPLES

KATHLEEN MACLAURIN

"If an army does not reflect the values and composition of the larger society that nurtures it, it invariably loses the support and allegiance of that society."[1]

INTRODUCTION

In order to remain accountable and responsible to the nation that supports them, militaries in democratic societies, and in particular the Canadian Forces (CF), must foster values that are compatible with those of the greater society, while at the same time remaining effective in achieving military missions. Furthermore, in order to meet its own personnel needs, the CF must draw from the largest possible pool of eligible, interested and motivated individuals in Canada's diverse population. This is necessary as a matter of organizational sustainability, but is also specifically required by the *Employment Equity Act of Canada* (EEA). Promulgated in 1995, the purpose of the EEA is to eliminate discriminatory employment practices for so-called "designated group members" (DGMs): women, Aboriginal persons, visible minorities and those with physical or other disabilities. As of 21 November 2002, the CF has in place special CF Employment Equity regulations to ensure that its workforce is representative of the Canadian population. As the CF must ensure compliance with the *Employment Equity Act* and its own internal regulations, as well as human rights compliance audits[2], defence leaders and policy makers require a high level of understanding of the values of DGMs – as a group and individually. This chapter seeks to highlight some of the value differences and similarities between the aboriginal (or indigenous) community and those of the military.

The chapter is based on historical and current literature, Department of National defence (DND) documents, and observa-

tion from this author's participation in various Aboriginal and
defence forums. Much of what follows is extracted from a larger
DND study on organizational values in the CF and Aboriginal
communities.[3] It seeks to generate further thought on the issue of
Aboriginal values vis-à-vis those of the military. This is
accomplished by examining issues surrounding value formation,
and value orientation, and by highlighting those values that are
mutually shared and promoted within the CF and the various
Aboriginal communities, as well as those that may be inconsistent
with different Aboriginal perspectives.

Neither the full historical narrative of Aboriginal peoples in Canada
nor the value frameworks that constitute all Aboriginal societies
can be addressed in a chapter of this length and scope, nor perhaps
in any single exploration. Thus, the value-related issues dealt with
below are not claimed to be exhaustive of those of all Aboriginal
communities nor are they considered necessarily representative of
the cultural complexity that now exists within and among them.
They are meant primarily to sensitize the military to the
importance of more closely examining the value-fit of various
Aboriginal groups with those of the military.

VALUES - THE CORNERSTONE OF BEHAVIOUR

Personal actions are influenced, to a considerable extent, by
cultural understandings of principles, beliefs, and values. Although
they may appear collectively linear, culture, beliefs, and values
should not be confused with one another. The relationship between
values and culture may be represented by an iceberg: the
behaviours that are normally associated with a given culture would
make up the visible top portion of the iceberg, while the sizable
hidden portion would consist of those beliefs, principles, and values
that influence cultural behaviour. Our principles, beliefs, and values
are major contributors to our culture, which in turn determines our

perceptions, attitudes, expectations, language, interactions, and patterns of existence. Beliefs are imbued with "ethics" – basic understandings of right and wrong – while values are socially constructed sets of ideals.[4]

As values may vary from one society to another, so may they vary, as an individual construct, from one person to the next. Values are deeply held beliefs about the ideal way to live one's life, but what constitutes *ideal* in any given society is entirely constructed by that society. Models of ideal conduct in a given society are generally introduced through the social interaction of its members, who internalize those values as part of their identities. What constitutes desirable conduct, however, is not static, and it differs substantially across cultural lines.[5]

From an Aboriginal perspective, values are conceptualized in terms of the ideal or desirable, as above, but what is *desired* finds greater clarity than we would find among those whose roots are in the Western European tradition. At the most basic level, values govern one's understanding of facts and truth and constitute the mechanisms used to observe the reality of one's world. In general, values are the means by which individuals pattern and use their energy to achieve a *balanced existence*.[6]

It is the belief of many Aboriginal peoples that without a balance between personal values and external behaviour, it is impossible for human beings to develop to their full potential.[7] "The whole system of Indigenous thought is a reflection of this balance of mind, body and spirit. The mechanisms by which this is delivered on a day-to-day basis are geared to ensuring that the balance is maintained."[8]

Consequently, the dissimilarity between values espoused by bureaucratic organizations, such as the military, and those promoted by Aboriginal communities could, at times, simply result from different value definitions. It is important to consider this factor when contemplating differences in value orientations between or among groups. Various deeply ingrained value sets shared between Aboriginal communities and the military may be similar to one another (e.g., honour, wisdom, loyalty, respect) but may be singly and collectively internalized for vastly dissimilar reasons. For example, where courage within Aboriginal communities may be a value intrinsic to their historic survival (e.g., against environmental threats, etc.), the rationale may well be different for members of a military organization. Also, whereas Canadians of European descent tend to encourage values that focus on ideal conduct in a given society, Aboriginal communities cultivate those values most likely to bring about a balanced existence. Thus, it is important to know the basis (most frequently found in historical processes) on which values are conceptualized and defined.

A SNAPSHOT OF HISTORICAL IMPACTS ON ABORIGINAL VALUES

The values and status of Aboriginal people in Canada today have been influenced by their environment and changed by contact with early European "settlers". Interpretations of the nature and extent of this impact vary. On the one hand, the federal government has been accused of perpetrating "cultural genocide" against Canada's Aboriginal peoples; this is based on evidence of an historic, systematic and sustained attack to extinguish the latter's ethno-cultural identities that only recently has abated. On the other hand, not all contact with the so-called early settlers of Canada could be characterized as disagreeable for Aboriginal peoples, owing to the substantial resources they obtained through trading with them.[9] However, this is an economic advantage that may have been more apparent than real.

The present conditions experienced by Aboriginal peoples in Canada are primarily the result of various circumstances and relations that have existed over the past several hundred years, beginning with prolonged social interaction between Aboriginal peoples and early European settlers. Value systems of Aboriginal communities and their members have been unavoidably influenced by both the conditions of the time and the interaction that occurred in that historical context. Communities thus reflect a mixture of traditional (from an Aboriginal perspective) and contemporary (Western societal) ideologies, and, to a considerable extent, so do their members, who have one foot planted in each world. These adaptations have evolved over time and are the outcomes of a particularly tumultuous past.[10]

Contact with Europeans had immediate and dire costs for the Aboriginal peoples of North America. They were active in the European efforts towards settlement, the fur trade, and warfare between the French and the English colonizers, activities that had significant impact on the integrity of their existing value orientations. In the Europeans' quests for land and dominion, their eventual desire to fully assimilate Aboriginal peoples drastically reduced the Aboriginal population[11] and changed their cultural communities and their values forever. Demographically, the Aboriginal population in Canada was reduced to a tenth of its original size owing to their lack of immunity to life-threatening communicable diseases brought by the settlers to the new colonies. Politically, Aboriginal people were marginalized and forced from their home territories, put on reserves, and excluded from the economic mainstream, where they had once been prominent traders and economic actors.

Accordingly, Aboriginal nations descended into poverty and became dependent on the Canadian government and its rigid, often discriminatory, regulations.[12] To a great extent, traditional languages were lost, destroyed, or weakened and, with them, the oral tradition of relaying history and culture. Cultural communication was undermined, the roots of the original Aboriginal population were damaged, and the poverty and destruction of traditional social controls resulted in tragic social conditions. In recent years, the Aboriginal population has outgrown the reserve areas set aside for them by the federal government, and many Aboriginal people are now navigating the complexities of an urban existence[13] The average age of the Aboriginal population is 10 years lower than the 35.4 year average of the general Canadian population.[14] The overall result is that Aboriginal cultural legacies, customs, and conventions have dissipated; social values and individual principles have become altered and variable. To a large extent, this has introduced tension and disruption into contemporary Aboriginal relations, both among themselves and with the non-Aboriginal community and institutions, such as the military.

WHY SHOULD THE CANADIAN FORCES EXPLORE ABORIGINAL VALUES?

The Canadian military advocates that the full contribution of all members must be appreciated and recognized to ensure their continued sense of worth and their commitment to the institution. For example, the CF *Principle of Fairness and Equity* policy claims to be "founded upon the acknowledgment of the dignity and worth of the individual". The development and application of the policy recognizes individual attributes, strengths and differences. As well, this facilitates timely response, transparency, and active acknowledgment of the individual right to privacy.[15] It is vital, then, that the CF determine, acknowledge, and understand those values that establish a sense of worth among Aboriginal service members while, at the same time, recognizing the differences in those cultural values which determine behaviour. Thus, it will be necessary to explore values that are compatible and identify those that might be potentially conflicting.

From this point, as far as operational effectiveness will allow, human resources policy must be proactive in recognizing the significance of cultural values among Aboriginal people and other diverse communities in Canada, and must strive to integrate, rather than assimilate, these principles into Canadian Forces standards. Norton and McKee state: "accommodating diversity is not simply assimilating diverse groups into the organization".[16] Rather, "it must involve a process of "mutual accommodation" where both the organization and the persons entering it must change and adapt."[17] However, the responsibility of deciding "what kinds, and how much accommodation can be made, while still meeting its operational goals", very much lies with the Canadian Forces.[18]

In keeping with the principles of fairness and equity, it is important that an increased awareness of the value orientations of Aboriginal people be developed within the Department of National Defence (DND) and the CF, so as to recognize their full potential significance for serving Aboriginal members. Furthermore, the principle of mutual accommodation necessitates a shared understanding and adaptation to members' behaviours, within reasonable operational constraints. As an appreciation of the behaviour that stems from identifiable value orientations grows, the CF should be in a better position to identify and initiate strategies to recruit and retain Aboriginal people.

VALUE ORIENTATIONS

Many Aboriginal communities across Canada share a number of broad value orientations. These are general ideologies – rather than specific, fully internalized morals and ethics – within each community that influence the behaviour of the individuals.

Underlying values also shape CF culture and the actions of its members. Although change is occurring as multicultural groups increase in Canada, we assume at this point that, given the political and religious history of this nation, the espoused values of the CF as a whole are primarily Euro-Judeo-Christian in their origin and thus differ from Aboriginal societies. Moreover,

> [Since] the CF is a voluntary service, it is implied that those most attracted to a military career will form the bulk of senior personnel, while the very nature of organized military life further suggests that its core group will tend to share a number of common characteristics. One must account for the fact that the military, more than many other types of human institutions, has maintained itself by adherence to and perpetuation not only of organizational but also of social traditions.[19]

These are the social traditions of a primarily British European ancestry. British European ancestry has traditionally made up over 60 percent of the CF personnel and nearly 75 percent of the officer ranks in the CF. In the early 1970s, for example, as many as 80 percent of navy personnel alone could trace their ethnic origins to the British Isles.[20] It is crucial that human resources planning, if it is to be successful, recognizes and acknowledges any fundamental incompatibilities between the European and Aboriginal social value frameworks and potential areas of conflict, since these are bound to act as barriers and challenges to the recruitment and retention of Aboriginal people.

COMPARING VALUES: POTENTIAL COMPATIBILITY

A number of value orientations nurtured within Aboriginal communities are similar, if not parallel, to the espoused values of the CF. It is on these areas that the CF might focus to achieve success in the further development of policy and programs affecting Aboriginal personnel. It is likely that the recruitment and, especially, the retention of Aboriginal personnel will be positively affected by recognition and acknowledgment within the Canadian Forces of compatible value orientations.

Perhaps most importantly, the spiritual orientations of Aboriginal and non-Aboriginal people acknowledge the existence of a higher being who is credited with the creation of earth and its beings. For much of Western society, that being is often of a Christian origin but, given that Aboriginal peoples acknowledge and nurture a belief in the "Creator", there is a similarity between the faiths. Each such being is conceived of as being somehow attached to the world that they have created, and powerful in their capacity as the creator of all earthly beings. For this reason, the value of a "higher being" is compatible, and provided that there are no distinctions as to whom individuals are devoted, the values themselves are harmonious.

Similarly, although much social emphasis is placed upon individualism and personal achievement in non-Aboriginal society, the CF places considerable emphasis on group effort and group achievement. The value of group effort and social accomplishment is commonly held by Aboriginal nations with respect to survival and sharing, and is quite well matched to the operational team approach of the CF. The idea that *deliberate* socialization is shared by both societies is decidedly prevalent, either through informal modelling in Aboriginal communities or through more rigorous formal integration, such as those aimed at inculcating acceptable conduct and behaviour or imparting specific skill-culture sets in CF training. One of the major intents of organizational socialization, in both the CF and in Aboriginal communities, is to have individuals identify themselves as integral parts of the community or institution, thereby ensuring that they will be able to capably perform the required roles within each context. Hence, although the *processes* by which socialization occurs within each group are markedly different, the *value* of socialization itself is quite similar.

Another specific parallel value falls within the rubric of transmission of information and guidance through storytelling and mythology. The transmission of information orally continues to occupy an important space within Aboriginal communities, where storytelling is the means by which individuals establish themselves as holders of wisdom and tradition, and is the method used by traditional societies to pass on important lessons, morals, and teachings. Several studies have been completed regarding the place of storytelling in the military, each defining the importance of this tradition. Storytelling in the military is intentionally comprised of tacit guidance and is a means of identifying correct and incorrect behaviour. Ann Irwin suggests that:

> by telling stories, the NCO [Non Commissioned Officer] reinforces both personal and competent authority. Personal authority is reinforced through the act of storytelling itself, as it is by its very nature an intimate and nurturing act. When he tells stories about his own shortcomings and mistakes he increases the level of trust which is such an important aspect of personal authority... Through storytelling the NCOs are confirmed and reinforced as the upholders of tradition.[21]

The existence of medical and health professionals within the organization or community is an important component of both military and Aboriginal life. It reaffirms the notion that these communities are cohesive, fully functional organizations unto themselves with full capacity to tend to the physical and other health needs of their members. Although the methods and resources for medical care introduced in the western context may differ slightly from those traditionally accepted within Aboriginal communities, the concept of medical and health training within the community *for* the community is similar. This also presents potential opportunities for Aboriginal people to receive medical and health-related training and take these skills home to their communities after having served in the CF. Thus, service in the military health care fields might prove to be a very attractive idea for Aboriginal peoples who place significant value on community health care in their home areas – as well they often need to do, owing to the gross neglect that they often have suffered over the years at the hands of well-meaning but inept government and other regulatory officials.

Finally, discipline, honour, and tradition are all clear value agreements in the CF and across Aboriginal communities. It should be reiterated, however, that each of these value stances has a different meaning to the communities or individuals that possess them, and they also may be embedded within that community or internalized by a person for a variety of specific reasons. They may operate in such a manner as to create conflict in specific circumstances, but they are nonetheless compatible value stances that are established in both the CF and Aboriginal communities.

EXPLORING VALUES: POTENTIAL CONFLICTS

An exploration of complementary values naturally exposes value orientations that are inconsistent, and even conflicting, between the CF and Aboriginal societies. These differing value orientations have the potential to create tension and discord among CF members and could preclude the involvement of prospective Aboriginal enrollees. The values themselves may or may not be alterable, but it is important that CF human resources agents be aware that tension may arise out of such differences. Respect for differences and acknowledgment of the dignity of others must be created within an organization if the values of other groups are to be recognized and respected. Without acceptance of such differences, it is difficult to implement policies that will accommodate them within an organizational setting. The striking dissimilarity between the value orientations of Aboriginal and non-Aboriginal people is most prevalent with respect to the Aboriginal peoples' circular conception of existence, which would appear to be entirely inconsistent with the triangular, hierarchical concept fostered by non-Aboriginal peoples and, most emphatically, by militaries. This is not merely a case of religious orientation; indeed, it is a reflection of the hierarchical makeup of most of Western society, and its institutions. The pyramidal system is entirely inconsistent with the Aboriginal sense of non-dominion over resources, be they natural (earth), financial, or physical (material goods).

Furthermore, whereas most Aboriginal communities consider all life forms equal, in Western society deference patterns emerge out of its fundamentally unequal makeup. Such deferential behaviour does not exist to the same extent within Aboriginal communities, where social inequality is not valued, but universal respect is most highly valued. Native common law promotes self-determination and self-realization that leave no room for social or interpersonal inequality.

This structure would suggest a potentially crippling impact on personnel relations in that the CF presumes an intrinsic inequality, if only in status and position, between individuals in the military. According to Donna Winslow:

> In the military, soldiers and officers find themselves in an orderly structure which determines who they are and what they do in addition to what their obligations to others are. There is a clear distinction between soldiers and officers. This separation is maintained through the military hierarchy and is even maintained informally, i.e., they rarely socialize with each other.[22]

While inequality between human beings is not a recognized practice in many Aboriginal communities (although specific reverence patterns exist for esteemed elders, in keeping with the significance of universal respect for the wisdom that is assumed to come with age and experience), there is a strong possibility that Aboriginal people may find the formalized military system oppressive, difficult to understand, and inherently unfair. A feeling of isolation and segregation in the face of organizational inequality may result, and this might prevent some Aboriginal personnel from fully "buying in" to the military "system".

Furthermore, in many Aboriginal communities an ethic of "non-interference" originates from the very common and very deeply held value of true freedom. It is an ethic barring the interference of Aboriginal peoples in the rights, privileges, and activities of others and precluding any "forced advice" from Aboriginal peoples. There exists a moral principle within most Aboriginal communities that prohibits direct, hurtful criticism of another individual – a tendency that contradicts the very nature of most non-Aboriginal institutions.

The CF, however, is an institution built on superiors' (and especially superior officers') imposition of guidance and orders upon its personnel. This formalized direction and "interference" on the part of superiors may contribute to many of the difficulties faced by Aboriginal personnel in terms of open, free communication and rank relations. An avoidance of offering direct advice through orders and various other means, or even a direct evasion of giving orders, indicates an underlying discomfort with this type of behaviour. An intrinsic disposition towards reticence and taciturnity, based on this ethic of non-interference, may manifest itself in a preference for silence on occasions when a response is expected and, indeed, called for within the military context. For the Aboriginal member, the result may well go beyond simple discomfort to feelings of isolation and social exclusion. It may become the source of conflict in the workplace and possibly even negatively impact the evaluation of Aboriginal members' potential by superiors or supervisors, with obvious consequences for individual training, promotion, and career development. This is likely to be a factor contributing to the very low representation of Aboriginal personnel in the CF officer corps and among senior non-commissioned officers.

The value of freedom, in the form of non-aggression, in some Aboriginal communities is occasionally linked to "avoidance" behaviours. For example, in some Aboriginal nations, direct eye contact is considered to be a sign of hostility or invasion and directly contradicts the principle of non-aggression that is prominent in some Aboriginal communities. The avoidance of shaking hands upon first encounter, a traditional welcoming gesture in Western society and one actively practised within the CF is another expression of the Aboriginal value of non-antagonism.

Stemming from the same circular versus pyramidal models, administrative matters are fraught with inconsistencies between Aboriginal and non-Aboriginal communities. For example, administration of public affairs by Aboriginal nations is built on a consensus model that is entrenched in the same circular model outlined previously. Management of public affairs in non-Aboriginal societies is most often, however, configured in the same hierarchical pyramid structure as existence and human standing, and it is certainly exhibited through the sometimes difficult and perplexing military operational context. Improving the accessibility and simplicity of the operational system may well appeal to the Aboriginal value of consensual decision-making, as rendering it more comprehensible should make Aboriginal members feel they have an informed voice in contributing to the operational process and objectives.

VALUES AND HUMAN RESOURCE POLICIES AND PRACTICES

Many evident themes emerge from entrenched CF human resource policies that may not fully recognize or accommodate different Aboriginal values and may also regularly have negative effects on the career development and retention of Aboriginal personnel. As a symbolic example, the commissioning scroll used in the appointment of commissioned officers and other such ceremonial occasions when allegiance to the Crown is called for may present a political conflict for those Aboriginal communities that do not recognize the Monarch as their sovereign and place no value in defending soil that is not their own. Indeed, the Aboriginal person may be more drawn to the United States military, where allegiance under all circumstances is to the nation and where the emphasis is placed on defending the earth that they occupy. This may be a contributing factor to the comparatively low representation of Aboriginal peoples in the CF officer or even the non-commissioned officer ranks, for example. There are, however, several Aboriginal nations throughout Canada that do indeed adhere to the notion of the sovereign monarchy and the leadership of England – in fact, First Nations communities have actually appealed to the Crown – and would thus not find the commissioning scroll or swearing allegiance to Her Majesty in conflict with their value systems.

Families are highly valued by Aboriginal people and putatively, as well, by the military – but there may be important differences in what is regarded as the meaningful family unit. Differences in definitions of what constitutes family amongst Aboriginal personnel and other military personnel are most visibly reflected in the issues surrounding compassionate leave policy, proximity to community and isolation policies. The CF compassionate leave policy offers assistance and support to those service personnel who have lost a member of their immediate family. The policy is governed by the following definition of immediate family:

"Immediate family" means a person with whom the officer or non-commissioned member is in a relationship (recognized marital relationship)... and any person who stands in one of the following relationships to the member or a person with whom the member is in a relationship recognized under article 1.075:

1. a child:
2. the father or mother and the spouse or partner of that person;
3. a brother or sister; and
4. a person who has undertaken the responsibilities and fulfilled the duties of a father or mother.[23]

Given the historical significance of the immediate "nuclear" family for most of the Canadian population, this policy does not appear to violate the value orientations of most CF members. However, given that many Aboriginals have an extended family system that makes no distinction between the immediate family and much of the surrounding community, this policy contradicts the internalized principles of most Aboriginal peoples. For example, there exists no definition for an aunt, uncle, or cousin in many Aboriginal communities. These persons, although biologically separated from the Aboriginal person and distinctly different relational categories, are socially accepted as mothers, fathers, brothers, and sisters of that person. The Aboriginal person is the child of the entire community and is expected to maintain a presence in the community, especially during times of grieving.

For this reason, an Aboriginal member may experience difficulty when required to distinguish between immediate and extended family for the purposes of CF bereavement leave. Indeed, such issues have been identified as contributors to the early release of

Aboriginal service members, a significant problem from the perspective of strategic human resource planning in the CF. Among Aboriginal CF members dealing with compassionate leave policy or other similar matters, the "situations were accompanied by increasing frustration, loneliness and continuous thoughts of their perceived obligations to their family... The ultimate solution was to return to the environment in which they felt most comfortable."[24] This type of experience also reflects the relative inflexibility of CF human resource policies and practices. Amendments to the compassionate leave policy, so as to better accommodate Aboriginal members, should be seriously considered.[25]

The ability to return to their homes often has high value for many Aboriginal peoples, given that their extended family, spiritual direction, cultural grounding, and traditional hunting grounds are regularly located in and around these areas. The CF's tendency and need to post personnel at considerable distances from their homes presents a significant difficulty for some Aboriginal people, and may serve to reduce the probability of their enrolment and/or retention. In a 1995 attrition study that consisted of interviewing current and previous Northern Native Entry Program (NNEP) personnel, it was noted that Aboriginal candidates who were interviewed after release from the CF frequently made reference to preoccupation with thoughts of home and family or sought input from their home community in decision-making. References were also made to failure on course training as a preferable option to voluntary withdrawal [from service] because the former resulted in a paid trip home. Several also expressed a preference for a posting location as close to home as possible to provide greater access to family and community.

As well, the CF policy on "Isolation Allowance" does not address the physical and mental isolation of Aboriginal personnel posted to larger, southern urban areas that are isolated from their remote northern communities. Instead, the CF Administrative Order 20-4 (replaced by DAOD 5003-6)[26] identifies environment, living cost differential, and fuel and utilities as the rationales used in selecting and rating posts for isolation allowance. In addition, serving members (and accompanying family members) at an "isolated post" are entitled to enhanced leave travel assistance (LTA) to allow them to proceed on leave "without being subjected to excessive expenditures".[27] Aboriginal members often "are socially and geographically isolated from their home communities at the same time that they are experiencing the cumulative challenges of cultural, organizational, and occupational learning".[28] However, they are not entitled to enhanced leave travel provisions unless they are serving at a CF-defined "isolated post". It has been recommended that CF policy be examined with a view to providing greater access to home, especially during the first three years of service. For example, annual leave entitlements, LTA, and isolated travel allowance policies could be reviewed to ensure that NNEP candidates are given access to home in a form that is equitable to that of their southern peers serving in isolated and non-isolated areas of Canada. In addition, posting policy could be reviewed to ensure that posting preferences are given due consideration, especially when it would provide greater access to the candidate's home.[29]

In combination with the above factors, Aboriginal people in the CF often cite their tendency to avoid others by their own choice, due to the perceived potential for their ideas to be ridiculed or disregarded by authority figures. They have thus reported feeling isolated in CF units because of an inability to communicate with others like themselves, and being "cut off" from their own culture, family, and community. Their world views are challenged, and in most cases, changed to suit their new military environment. It is the pervasive isolation from their home community combined with their aversion to creating conflict that underlies this change.

CF human resource approaches for enhancing workplace relations, such as policies relating to grievances, harassment, and discrimination, may not represent viable options for Aboriginal people. Recent data indicates that these policies are often unsuccessful among serving Aboriginal members, owing to the potentially strong aversion among Aboriginal people to interfering with another's freedom, as discussed previously. Aboriginal peoples will often display a strong aversion to infringing on the freedom of another, even when instructed to do so by policy. As author Rupert Ross, an academic who has studied and lived with Aboriginal communities in northern Ontario has expressed it:

> True to traditional ethics prohibiting the criticism of others or interference in their choices, they [Aboriginal peoples] do not pass open judgement on what we do to ourselves, except in the environmental context where they too are equally affected. They do not presume to tell us what to do, as we have told them since first contact....Many Native people think our ways of doing things create more problems than they solve, especially when they increase individual anger, alienation, selfishness and envy..."[30]

The inherent potential to create conflict that underlies the formal complaint process is understandably avoided by those Aboriginal people who nurture a "non-interference" worldview. Thus complaint mechanisms do not seem to work as well for Aboriginal members as it may for others. For example, when non-Aboriginal advisors or investigators examine a case concerning harassment or discrimination, their inadequate cultural understanding often means that the guidance they provide is inappropriate for Aboriginal members. Despite their use of available complaint mechanisms, Aboriginal service members may still feel unsupported and misunderstood, since they perceive that many supervisors do not attempt to understand the cultural differences intrinsic to their case. They consistently report a sense of feeling "absolutely alone" in their situation.[31]

Experienced Aboriginal service members and civilian employees alike suggest the inclusion of an educated, cultural assistant to aid in the resolution of the complaint issues. This would ensure that support for the plaintiff originates from a cultural perspective understood by skilled individuals and that assessments of the situation are not biassed in favour of the values and practices of the larger organization. Furthermore, the component of the complaint policy regarding the position of the "Harassment Advisor" fails to comprehensively address the issue of differences in value orientation. It simply requires the Harassment Advisor to consult with cultural advisors during the mediation process, with no requirement that they be trained in cultural differences. This applies to all members of the complaint process, including immediate supervisors and harassment investigators.[32]

The appropriate use of Elders within the CF is encouraged, and some locations have recently appointed a "Base Elder" to provide spiritual support to Aboriginal service personnel. Such an action, though well-intentioned, may well run counter to Aboriginal value orientations, since no single Elder can be expected to spiritually guide the variety of different Aboriginal groups within the CF. Given the vast dissimilarities among simple culture areas, an Aboriginal person could not be expected to adhere to any given Elder's interpretations of the world.[33] In instances like this, good intentions without appropriate awareness or consultation can have negative impacts on the experiences of serving Aboriginal people, with corresponding implications for lower motivation and retention in the CF.

CONCLUSION: BALANCING MILITARY ETHOS, VALUES, AND ORGANIZATIONAL REQUIREMENTS

The CF recognizes that servicemen and servicewomen are the basis of military operations and that they must adhere to the policies of the organization. Hence, a formalized ethos statement for all CF members[34] defines the institution vis-à-vis other institutions and groups in Canadian society and attempts to shape individual attitudes and beliefs into a pattern of behavior that leads to high levels of cohesion, dedication, and esprit de corps. It is comprised of attitudes that are oriented to fulfilment of the military mission and the willing subordination of one's self to a higher goal, as well as to an organization that is greater than oneself. It essentially attempts to inculcate in members those essential moral and physical attributes that will shape individual attitudes and beliefs into a pattern of desired behaviour.[35]

Essentially, the military ethos is intended to provide individual military members with a clear understanding of the fundamental moral purpose of their service, and it reflects the four core components of the CF: warrior spirit, ethical values, military values, and a reflection of Canadian society. In terms of the latter objective, it is the intention of the ethos statement to respect the dignity and rights of individuals, embrace national ideals, and provide an equal opportunity for all Canadians.

Nevertheless, the question remains as to whether some Aboriginal people may be deterred from enlisting in the military for fear that the objectives of the ethos statement would assimilate and extinguish their own particular value orientations or give rise to value stances that are in direct opposition to their own. However, given that Canada is a multicultural nation with vastly different cultural customs, it should certainly not be expected that the CF could enact every national ideal into unique policies and practices.

Indeed, the institution must maintain commitment to specific areas of "vital ground" to ensure that its operational integrity and effectiveness are not compromised.

Vital ground includes those value orientations that are essential elements of military organizations. It is thought by some that there exists a pervasive erosion of fundamental military values in the face of a diversified organizational structure; that elemental values essential to effective operations, as well as the character, morale, and quality of the military, are being damaged by gradual changes that encourage diversity and reflect civil society within the CF.[36] Interviews reveal that a minority of members believe that employment equity, special entry programs, cultural integration, and other initiatives serve to undermine the integrity and true mission of the military. Their view is consistent with the position that:

> a democracy cannot defend a democracy. It takes an authoritarian system, one with a clear hierarchy where orders are given and things are accomplished in a specific way...In order to act aggressively, you have to be aggressive, you have to possess within you the necessary values to be able to kill someone if you have to. But in the civilian Canadian society, these values are unacceptable.[37]

The military ethos encourages the values of duty, integrity, loyalty, and courage – all seemingly essential and related to the fundamental requirement of unlimited liability of CF members. Among other things, such values also underlie the responsibility and legitimacy of taking a human life in the defence of Canadian values, if necessary.[38] In the minds of some, redefining the military as a mainline corporate institution, rather than one with a unique operational mission to defend Canada, is a deceptive endeavour. On the other hand, the military needs to question traditional notions of operational *effectiveness* and social isolation that appear dysfunctional to overall military *organizational* effectiveness.

To better accommodate Aboriginal peoples and thus make the military a more attractive option for them, the CF will need to undertake planned change on the value dimension. This would more fully meet the requirements of the *Multiculturalism Act* and the *Employment Equity Act* and, at the same time, better address operational and organizational needs. Thus the challenge to change a historically held, institutionally perpetuated impression of Aboriginal peoples is presented to the CF. The desire to create a values-based workplace that welcomes a diverse cross-section of Canadians is unlikely to be realized without a concentrated effort to challenge and transform misconceptions about the abilities of Aboriginal peoples and their place in the military. A genuine attempt must be made to understand the issues from the various Aboriginal perspectives. At the same time, the CF should examine the extent to which the reinforcement of values and enhancement of cultural identities within individual persons and ethnically diverse units can strengthen force cohesion. Some attempt must be made to draw clear lines between the level of cultural reinforcement that will improve force cohesion, and the point at which the enhancement of cultural identities would potentially mitigate the effectiveness of operational units.

Whether or not individual Aboriginal people have been directly affected by past injustices, the concept of "tribal memory" captures the broader impact that these injustices have had across Aboriginal communities.[39] This highlights the need to understand the experiences of individual Aboriginal people within the context of their cultural history. If the true intention of the CF is to create an environment where Aboriginal people will adapt and thrive, policy makers should re-examine apparently incompatible human resource policies and ensure that future policy initiatives are developed in concert with Aboriginal communities. It is this type of awareness and inclusion that is most likely to enhance mutual accommodation between Aboriginal people and the CF.

NOTES

1   David Bercuson, *Significant Incident* (Toronto: McClelland and Stewart, 1996).

2   Director Military Gender Integration and Employment Equity (DMGIEE)

3   MacLaurin, Kathleen, *Organizational Values in the Canadian Forces and Aboriginal Communities – Contemporary Perspectives on Conflict and Compatability*, Ottawa, 2001, Department of National Defence

4   Michael Adams, *Sex in the Snow*, Penguin Books of Canada, 1999

5   Jodie Bopp, Micheal Bopp, Lee Brown, and Phil Lane Junior, *The Sacred Tree* (Alberta, Four Worlds International Institute for Human and Community Development, 1984)

6   Ibid.

7   R. Neil, *Voice of the Drum* (Brandon MA: Kingfisher Publications, 2000), quoted in *Our Responsibility to the Seventh Generation, Indigenous Peoples and Sustainable Development*, L Morisette Clarkson and G. Gegallet (Winnipeg: International Institute for Sustainable Development, 1992).

8   Rupert Ross, *Dancing with a Ghost - Exploring Indian Reality* (Markham ON: Octopus Publishing Group, 1992).

9   Neil McDonald, *Working with Aboriginal Peoples - A Guide to Effective Cross Cultural Communication* (Ottawa: Cross Cultural Consulting, 2001).

10   Charlie Taiowsakarere Hill, A Course to Increase Awareness about Aboriginal Native American Cultures (Ottawa consultation: 2001).

11   MacLaurin, 2002, *Organizational Values in the Canadian Forces and Aboriginal Communities* (2)

12   Paradoxically, the same government that created this reliance later called for the legislative independence of Aboriginal peoples in its 1968 White Paper

13   Statistics Canada, *The Daily - January 13th, 1988-1996 Census: Aboriginal Data* (Ottawa, 1996).

14   Canadian Forces, *HR Strategy 2020: Facing the People Challenges of the Future* (Ottawa, draft April 2002).

15   S. Norton and B. McKee, *The Importance of Values Research for Strategic HR in the Canadian Forces* (Ottawa: National Defence, Directorate of Strategic Human Resource Coordination, 2001).

16   Cross-Cultural/Multicultural Associates Inc., *A Conceptual Framework for Achieving Diversity and Equity in the Canadian Forces*, Technical Note 00-2, (Ottawa: Department of National Defence, Directorate of Human Resources Research and Evaluation, 1997).

17   Ibid.

18   Morris Janowitz, *On Military Ideology* (Rotterdam, Rotterdam University Press, 1971).

19   Ibid.

20   Anne Irwin, *Canadian Infantry Platoon Commanders and the Emergence of Leadership* (Unpublished master's thesis, University of Calgary, Calgary, AB, 1993).

21   Donna Winslow, *The Canadian Airborne Regiment in Somalia - A Socio-cultural Inquiry* (Ottawa: Minister of Public Works and Government Services Canada, 1997).

22   *Queen's Regulations and Orders*, Chapter 209, Section 51.

23   Karen Davis, *Northern Native Entry Program Attrition Monitoring: A Preliminary Evaluation*, Technical Note 12/05 (North York, ON: Canadian Forces Personnel Applied Research Unit, 1995).

24   Ibid.

25   Ibid.

26   Defence Administrative Orders and Directives, 5003-6, Compassionate Status, Compassionate Posting and Contingency Costs Moves for Personal Reasons, 2002-02-08

27   Ibid., 209-15.

28   Davis, *Northern Native Entry Program Attrition Monitoring*: 2.

29   Ibid.: 3

30   Rupert Ross, *Dancing with a Ghost - Exploring Indian Reality* (Markham ON: Octopus Publishing Group, 1992).

31   Defence Aboriginal Advisory Group (Consultation, Ottawa, 2001).

32   Ibid.

33   The ethos statement is currently being revised; broader cultural inclusion is one of several issues under consideration.

34   National Defence, *Duty with Honour The Profession of Arms in Canada*. NDID Number: A-PA-005-000/AP-001, (Ottawa, 2003).

35   Interviewee cited in *The Canadian Airborne Regiment in Somalia*, Winslow, 2.

36   Winslow, *The Canadian Airborne Regiment in Somalia*, 2

37   Interviewee cited in T*he Canadian Airborne Regiment in Somalia*, Winslow, 42.

38   National Defence, *Duty with Honour The Profession of Arms in Canada*. NDID Number: A-PA-005-000/AP-001, (Ottawa, 2003).

39   McDonald; *Working with Aboriginal Peoples*: 2.

DIVERSITY:
CONDITIONS FOR AN ADAPTIVE, INCLUSIVE MILITARY

FRANKLIN C. PINCH

INTRODUCTION

This volume began by suggesting that the cultural and social diversity found in most Western and many non-Western societies is reflected in the human resource management policies of the militaries concerned. Harries-Jenkins has made the convincing argument that older, conservative, male-dominated models (e.g., the Institutional model and the warrior model) and their underlying assumptions have been overtaken by a new "diversity model" that is more in keeping with current reality. Most of the foregoing chapters deal with the barriers that still exist to accommodating this new reality. In a sense, all of these chapters attribute differences in social and cultural values to the resistance to continuing change. They also suggest that, to a considerable extent, we are still captives of older ideas about how the military should deal with differences in ethno-cultural and social groups that reside in society, including women and aboriginal people.

Despite the progress that has been made, most militaries still have difficulty encompassing the full potential of their host populations and transforming internal cultural and social patterns, values, norms, and beliefs that place some members at a disadvantage on the basis of their ascriptive characteristics. This chapter picks up on Harries-Jenkins' discussion on the conceptual and policy-related evolution of gender diversity. It briefly recaps the current situation with reference to models of change and resistance that have influenced policy over the past half-century and then offers comment on the conditions under which diversity-management policies are most likely to bring progress.

BACKGROUND

As Morris Janowitz recognized in *The Professional Soldier*,[1] the transformation to a much more socially and culturally *heterogeneous* armed force in the U.S. was already well under way in the 1950s. This was simply an internal reflection, both structurally and in policy, of demographic, socio-cultural, and technological changes in civilian society. Changes of this type have continued up to the present across many militaries.[2] Of course, in the U.S., racial integration of Afro-Americans started in the 1950s and, despite major setbacks, has evolved in a positive way overall.[3] In Canada, the less obvious and somewhat less problematic parallel involved integrating Canadian francophones into the armed forces and, later, responding to the formal policies of multiculturalism.

In the meantime, as noted elsewhere in this volume, Western societies have become increasingly diverse; but the military, along with other traditional institutions, has often failed to apprehend and respond to these trends until faced by human resource management crises or forced to do so by legal measures.[4] National legislative support has often been lacking – a key part of what Harries-Jenkins has referred to as "macro policy". However, to a considerable extent, these have been deficiencies in strategic military leadership: in particular, as suggested by Leuprecht in Chapter Six, long-term planning decisions that did not take account of critical social and demographic trends.

Moreover, military leadership has typically eschewed change initiatives perceived as "social innovation", most especially in regard to gender and sexual orientation. As David Segal has noted, military leaders have resisted virtually every type of social change by arguing that it would have a deleterious effect on cohesion and operational effectiveness.[5] This has included the integration of women and various minorities.[6] The apparently obsessive concern over disruptions to cohesion and operational effectiveness – touched upon in this volume by Harries-Jenkins and Davis and McKee – became associated with the "operational imperatives" model, which focused primarily on the traditional war-fighting role of the military, its uniqueness in terms of its mandated mission, and the relatively rigid *status quo* conditions that arguably were needed to sustain it. This was the "divergence" position, a normative argument that held the military should be both separate and different from its host society in terms of its culture, norms, values, beliefs, attitudes, and so on. The proponents of this view have drawn support from Samuel Huntington's *The Soldier and the State*,[7] which provided the intellectual and moral opposition to a military that attempted to encompass the norms of liberal-democratic society. In fact, Huntington linked civilian control of the military (always a concern in democratic societies when there is a large standing force) and professionalism of the officer corps to a conservative, clearly demarcated military institution, insulated from the influences of society. This position could be seen as an advantage for military leadership because it presumably kept politicians and others from interfering in the internal affairs of the military. Also, it told the military to stick to its task – managing large-scale violence and visiting the same upon the nation's enemies, as and when legitimately called upon – and not to concern itself with matters political or social.

SOCIAL IMPERATIVES AND THE ADAPTIVE MILITARY

The other side of the argument was dubbed the "social imperatives" model.[8] This view recognized that – especially where the military had to rely on the human resource pool and the support of the public to sustain itself (which was true in virtually all Western-style democratic societies) – perforce there had to be a great deal of interpenetration and boundary permeability between the military and society. Indeed, this was repeatedly shown to be the case.[9]

Militaries in industrial society began to look quite similar to other large-scale employment organizations in many of their defining structural features (e.g., occupational distributions, management hierarchy), as well as in their change dynamics; that is, military and civilian organization were *converging*.

This was the "adaptive military" to which Janowitz referred and which he hypothesized in terms of the "constabulary" concept.[10] The latter would change the role of the military from one accustomed to using unlimited force to win the nation's wars, to one dedicated to using minimum force to forestall or prevent all-out nuclear war and to assist in maintaining global peace and stability. The emphasis on the military as a war-fighting machine was thereby broadened to include assistance in conflict resolution. As we now recognize, this entailed the development of additional specialized skills, not the least of which were the political and diplomatic skills of negotiation and interaction with multinational, multicultural, non-military parties. This conceptual shift did not sit well with military traditionalists, who rejected the constabulary concept as being too similar to a police role, albeit on a global scale. Further, the adaptive social changes following the Second World War, and most particularly through the 1960s and 1970s, raised alarm over the "civilianization" of the military, especially in the U.S. and Canada.[11] Even Janowitz, who never ruled out a war-fighting role but saw it being used to maintain global peace and stability, believed that the uniqueness of the military mission imposed limits to civilianization.[12] The civilianization thesis assumed acceptance of civilian social norms and values underlying greater heterogeneity in leadership and decision-making models within the military. Increasing diversity is consistent with the notion of the constabulary force, expansion of the military role, and civilianization – all issues with which military leadership has experienced difficulty.[13]

For Janowitz, adaptability to societal change was part of a natural and foreseeable evolution.[14] Societal change was to be confronted, not with alarm but with adaptive policies for change in structure and process that would ensure continuing civil-military integration. Where Janowitz departed from Huntington's early perspective (Huntington later softened his position) was in believing that external integration and civilian control were achieved by having the military thoroughly embedded in its host society.[15] There were two major connectives: that military leaders should become more attuned to political realities and pressures and that military members should be imbued with, not alienated from, the values and sensitivities of the society in which they resided. These are highly relevant to contemporary military diversity management, since they refer to the accountability demanded by human rights legislation (where it exists) and the general public. Moreover, where Huntington identified features of the "military mind" that differed from those of civilian society, Janowitz advocated development of "social consciousness" among military members – especially leaders – beginning with understanding of their own local environment but becoming progressively more global and cosmopolitan in reach and understanding.[16] Janowitz expressed some concerns about racial imbalances that appeared with greater Afro-American enrolment at the beginning of the all-volunteer force era in the U.S., primarily as a representational issue, and not in opposition to including minorities. While Janowitz was largely silent on the role of women in the military, the inclusion of minorities and women in the military, *in a meaningful* way, is quite consistent with his adaptive military stance.

As suggested by Gwyn Harries-Jenkins (Chapter 2), Charles Moskos actually encompassed the operational imperatives and social imperatives models in his conceptualization of the I/O models.[18] In so doing, he captured the tensions that exist between a military that is legitimized by traditional norms and one that is clearly linked to characteristics of civilian society, especially as they relate to commercial marketplace modes of commitment and interaction. While no military or separate service has been shown to represent either a pure Institutional or Occupational type, Moskos has warned of the deleterious implications of an operational military adopting an Occupational model. For example, he has argued against the full integration of women (he sees nothing wrong with partial integration) and *openly* gay and lesbian participants (which led to the "don't ask, don't tell" US policy), but he supports full racial integration for males and, by inference, other ethno-cultural groups.[19] We must also remember that Moskos' context is the US, and his views cannot necessarily be extended to other Western militaries. Although the U.S. has influenced allied defence establishments in significant ways, there are many reasons (including size and their role as the sole superpower) why the US forces cannot be taken as a model in the post-modern era.[20]

Recently, Moskos has used his I/O model to compare racial integration and women's integration in the U.S. He notes distinct differences that place women at a disadvantage (e.g., physical, privacy, sexual relations, and harassment). These apply especially to inclusion in ground combat, which he has tended not to support. His conclusion suggests that the Institutional model applies to Afro-American integration and the Occupational model to women's integration. What this means, at least in the US context, is that women's integration will ultimately be more successful in civilian organizations than in the military. This may well be the case, but there is considerable evidence to show that women still face substantial barriers to their success in all types of organizations, especially in management roles.[21]

Unlike Davis and McKee (Chapter Three), some analysts doubt the practicability of human resource philosophies, policies, programs, and practices to overcome the above-noted barriers to women's success in the operational combat environment of the army.[22] The physical strength and endurance concerns are relatively straightforward to deal with if *realistic* occupational physical selection standards are applied, even though, as Harries-Jenkins indicated (in Chapter Two), they may neither solve the problem of *tokenism*, where only small numbers of women meet the standards, nor reduce the need for senior female role models. Policy applications for the other issues involve changing the masculine cultural and interactive norms of "teeth arms" environments in general and the combat arms in particular. Institutional-model adherents would argue against this on the grounds of operational effectiveness. To do so is to ignore the degree to which gender roles and role definitions are socially constructed. For the military, as elsewhere, they are also reinforced by the masculine culture.[23] The question remains as to how far the military is willing to go in changing the structural relationships (i.e., transforming the social and cultural environment), which now favour men over women, and whether the retention of masculine, as opposed to gender-neutral, norms is essential to the effectiveness of military forces. This issue has yet to be seriously and objectively addressed.[24]

TOWARD AN INCLUSIVE MILITARY

Oppositional concepts or ideal types, such as the operational-imperatives versus the social-imperatives models or the Institutional versus the Occupational models, have been used to help clarify evolutionary trends or tendencies in the military. However, these have led to either/or arguments that have tended to portray in a negative light any movement away from traditional exclusionary stances of the military. Thus, recently, James Burk has questioned this oppositional way of thinking on the basis that social reality is better depicted as a balance between the social and the operational imperatives models.[25] Society needs an operationally effective military, but the all-volunteer military cannot exist in splendid isolation from its society. It must be attuned to the requirements of its civilian stakeholders. (Moskos would not object to this, since he sees both Institutional and Occupational tendencies at play in the militaries of post-modern society.) This reflects Charles Cotton's earlier view that a military has to be both internally and externally integrated on a number of dimensions, including the value and attitudinal dimensions.[26]

Nevertheless, the argument is not that military norms and values should depart significantly from those of civil society. Rather, *additional* value emphases are needed to support fulfilment of the role obligations of the unique military mission. These inhere in a military ethos that encompasses distinctive military value requirements (duty, honour, integrity, unlimited liability, etc.) and the predominant social values of society (respect for democratic traditions, human and equality rights, accommodation of religious and cultural differences, etc.). In both its recently published profession of arms manual and a draft leadership manual, the Canadian military has attempted to strike this internal-external integration balance.[27] One of the most prominent considerations in both documents is the positive value that is placed on the bilingual and multicultural nature of Canadian society and the accommodation of change and diversity that this situation implies for the Canadian military. It is on this basis that an inclusive model of the military profession emerges, with implications for both internal and external integration, that has yet to be realized.[28]

At this point in the evolution of the military, several conditions appear necessary to make it an inclusive organization that gives every eligible citizen an opportunity to participate in the defence of the nation and, more generally, in national and international security. If the experience of the last half-century is any indicator, pressure from citizens or difficulty in maintaining requisite personnel levels, in and of themselves, will not necessarily lead to an inclusive military system. Rather, democratic regimes, through their governments and elected officials and the majority of their citizens, must support the notion of an inclusive military: one free of discrimination against any minority (including women who are treated as a minority). The only justifiable reasons for discrimination are failure to meet basic eligibility standards and the inability to meet fair selection criteria that are clearly linked to the capacity to adapt to and perform one's duties in the military.

Political or government support falls into two categories. One is a multicultural policy that formally encourages the participation of groups that might otherwise be excluded from the activities that are controlled by the dominant social group. The second is legislation that clearly and specifically defines universal human and equality rights and the conditions under which they will obtain, along with adjudication and enforcement mechanisms that give such legislation "teeth". Few nations have a policy on multiculturalism, even when it appears necessary, whereas many have some sort of human or equality rights legislation that applies to the military institution, at least in a general sense.

The second requirement is active support by the military leadership. Military leaders have been slow to develop the change concepts and mechanisms to make diversity work in the military context. In fact, as noted, such change has actually been resisted or otherwise approached in a perfunctory, unsystematic, and half-hearted manner.[29] Nor is it enough to have direction from above without the development and implementation of a well-articulated strategic vision and an approach that provides the concepts, philosophies, policies, programs, and practices – and the other resources that go along with them – to ensure that the desired organizational change will occur. For example, Sorin's research on the French military (Chapter Four) indicates that the major national educational institution for military leaders was not adequately prepared to accept women and that this produced significant gender-based conflict. Leadership issues relevant to making progress in diversity management are further discussed below.

THE ROLE OF LEADERSHIP: LEADING PEOPLE AND THE INSTITUTION

As regards military leadership, Karol Wenek has recently produced a series of papers that have influenced the writing of the new leadership manual for the Canadian Forces.[30] In so doing, he has brought to bear, in a logical and integrated manner, a powerful foundation on which contemporary leadership should be based. Most of what he has produced is highly applicable to the leadership of change and diversity management. According to Wenek, leadership in the military has two major areas of responsibility: "leading people" and "leading the institution". Also, military leadership is "distributed", in the sense that leadership responsibilities are found and leadership influence may be exerted at all levels of the organization. Moreover, leaders at the higher levels must respond to both the external environment and the internal institution.

Wenek lays out the responsibilities and response modes of what might otherwise be called "interactive leadership". This pertains to all leaders, whether they are squad or section leaders, small-unit leaders, aircraft and ships' captains, formation commanders or, indeed, chiefs of service and defence staffs. All leadership positions require specific levels of leadership competence as the basis for making decisions. A basic requisite is that they will operate within the rule of law, which is bound by a legal framework that encompasses the laws of the land (including those that pertain to human rights, social equity, and social justice), the laws of armed conflict and international conventions pertaining thereto, along any with special codes of conduct applicable to dutifully and honourably serving their nation in the armed forces. In Canada, for example, the Code of Service Discipline, which applies specifically to the conduct of all military members, reflects many of the legal principles of fairness and justice that inform the Canadian legal and judicial systems.

Further, leadership involves developing trust with and among those for whom the leader has been given formal supervisory responsibility. To be effective, professional military leaders require the ability to treat all people with respect, fairness, honesty, and integrity and to be actively involved in the development, well-being, and progress of those for whom they have direct leadership responsibility. A positive role-modelling requirement is a substantial part of being a leader of people. It is to be undertaken seriously, deliberately, and in a selfless manner. Without the latter, it would be difficult to expect military members to make the sacrifices needed to fulfil the military mission in the face of risk to themselves or other team members. This does not mean that all persons are treated the same, because not all have the same abilities, competencies, or needs, so it is important to relate to the uniqueness of the people with whom the leader has direct responsibility. Since they may come from different cultural, racial, or social backgrounds, these differences must be taken into account, to the extent that they can be identified. None should feel devalued, left out, or marginalized on the basis of their ascriptive characteristics; all should feel they are capable of making – indeed are expected to make – their own unique contribution to the tasks associated with the mission, goals, and objectives of the military. Overall, this is a tall leadership order but certainly achievable, given that military leaders are among the most advantaged when it comes to training and development in technical and leadership aspects of their professional roles. The implications for dealing with diversity are obvious.

LEADING THE INSTITUTION

Wenek suggests that leading the institution with respect to the inclusion of diversity involves "strategic work" and, at a minimum, performance of several key leadership tasks. First, executive leaders must set the premise for change to a diversity model that will be reflected throughout the leadership and management structure. In order to do this, they must provide the vision and direction for such change, using inputs from the primary stakeholder groups, especially those who will be most directly affected by the change.

This is not just a bureaucratic task of setting top priorities and allocating funds. It must be one of creating the compelling case for change from *what was or is* to *what is to be*. To a considerable extent, it involves the social construction of meaning and identity or, at least, provision of the "idea" or conceptual basis on which change may occur. As to diversity, part of the task is to project some idea of what the "new" or ideal collective identity should be (i.e., what the more inclusive "we" should look like).

Second, senior leaders must make available the resources needed to develop the structures, processes, and mechanisms to support and implement desired change. Again, with respect to diversity management, these resources should include the assistance required to ensure the development of a shared identity that will encompass all the essential elements, projected as an inclusive "community of interest", integrated at the level of shared ethos.

Third, they must take an active role in leading and championing the change, through whatever communication and other means are available. They must insist upon involvement and buy-in throughout the leadership structure; this requires the use of educative means, the considerable power and influence of positive sanctions such as performance evaluations and promotion systems and, as a last resort, the use of negative sanctions, to ensure there will be no "recalcitrants" or sub-cultures that will oppose, obstruct, or disrupt the desired change process. Other important support tools to be developed are third-party adjudicative and complaint mechanisms and arrangements to resolve problems that occur at the margins of change; such problems, if not adequately handled, can bring positive change to a halt.

Fourth, executive/senior leaders must ensure that processes and outcomes are properly monitored and evaluated so as to facilitate the assessment of progress and to minimize backsliding. In this respect, it is important to use whatever legislative or other external oversight is available to effect reporting, from the unit level up the executive level. To facilitate progress, successes and failures must be rigorously analyzed and the root cause(s) of both identified; these results can then be used pedagogically and persuasively in comparative models, and in a highly publicized "lessons learned" format.

Finally, even though change toward an inclusive military system that accommodates diversity is likely to be top-down at the beginning, senior leaders must find ways to involve members at every level in the process by demonstrating that the change is in the best interests of themselves and the institution. This involves both leadership and management initiatives that highlight the moral, ethical, and utilitarian aspects of change.

As suggested, providing appropriate change leadership includes guiding the institution through development and/or adaptation of a comprehensive human resource management (HRM) system. The system must be based on a policy foundation, concepts, and research that focus on the task of finding workable solutions, rather than those trying to prove the appropriateness of past practices. The military has often been accused of fighting the last war instead of the one at hand. This is no less the case when it comes to HRM systems that are based on obsolete or dysfunctional philosophies, policies, programs, and practices. As suggested by Burk and Harries-Jenkins and noted above, the notions of operational and social imperatives, reflected in other oppositional models, have been overtaken by more explanatory ideas and concepts. These include diversity, inclusiveness, and accommodation of differences: the direction in which most Western militaries are evolving. An HRM philosophy based on inclusiveness and accommodation searches for ways to remove barriers to full participation of citizens and members, rather than ways to restrict their involvement and employment in the military.

DISTRIBUTED LEADERSHIP

Distributed leadership means that intermediate and lower-level leaders – those involved in face-to-face, day-to-day leadership in the military – are also responsible for reflecting the ethos of accommodation of differences, whether they be ethno-cultural, social, or individual. For example, one of the problems with implementing gender diversity has been that many leaders either did not believe that they carried the obligation to make integration work (or that they had a right not to accept women in their midst) or they lacked the necessary understanding, knowledge, and skills to assume effective leadership of change.

Distributed leadership – which includes both formal and informal leadership roles – has an important part to play in inculcating appropriate values, beliefs, norms, and attitudes in initial and subsequent socialization, from squad to unit to higher organizational levels. In terms of content and role modelling (now changing, though not quickly enough), traditionally designed military-socialization systems have often reflected the denigration and exclusion of other cultural and social groups and civilians in general. Women have been prime targets of denigration, especially in the labels given to male trainees who exhibited any signs of "weakness" or "deficiency" in early training and development. Various racial and cultural groups have also come in for negative epithets (especially in informal hazing and indoctrination ceremonies), as have homosexual males. As late as the 1990s, young Canadian soldiers reported indulging in hyper-heterosexual behaviours so as to demonstrate their "straightness" and masculinity to their peers.[31] On the other hand, the results of harassment surveys, such as those completed at the end of the twentieth century and summarized by Holden and Davis (Chapter Five), suggest that social acceptance of diversity is increasing in these four Anglo-American militaries, as well as in others.

As Sorin's research demonstrates, this does not mean that everything is sweetness and light, however, even in those nations that have made deliberate, concentrated attempts to change the situation. Analysis of qualitative responses to a Canadian diversity survey also found that a minority of Canadian Forces members were of the view that activities surrounding gender-diversity policies and processes detracted from the true *raison d'être* of a military force.[32] This serves to reinforce the continuing need for new models of socialization that emphasize norms of respect, inclusiveness, and accommodation of cultural, social, and individual differences.

COSTS AND BENEFITS OF DIVERSITY INCLUSIVENESS

Diversity management of an inclusive military workforce comes with costs. One of them is a significant level of added complexity to leadership and management roles and the systems that have to support them. To effectively implement the diversity model in the military requires a commitment of additional time and resources, and, at least at the outset, the disruption that comes from change and conflict between the dominant and incoming groups.[33] One of the major reasons for these costs is that the organization has been designed for the "mainstream" and not to accommodate incoming groups. There is no way around these costs if real change is to occur.

Nevertheless, it is also the case that women, representatives of racial and ethnic groups, and other minorities have borne a disproportionate share of both discomfort and conflict in the military, especially in the more "closed" operational segments. As MacLaurin's value comparisons between the military and aboriginals (Chapter Seven) remind us, we should expect both value congruence and value conflict between the military and ethno-cultural groups. Transition to a diversity model will most certainly involve culture clashes and value conflicts, which must be worked through, with appropriate models, policies, structures, and processes. For example, as both Harries-Jenkins and Davis and McKee suggest, the transition to gender diversity will not be complete until the cultural aspects of the combat masculine warrior model are sufficiently modified to give women their rightful place of comfort (see below).

The perceived need for diversity management and the manner in which it is approached in the military will continue to vary across nations and their militaries. According to Söeters and van der Meulen, in their review of case studies on nine countries,[34] there are at least five "reasons", which can be related to various national contexts, as to why diversity management should exist in armed forces. These include acknowledgment of social or cultural identity and basic civil rights; creation and maintenance of legitimacy with key stakeholders (politicians, employers and the general public); expansion of the pool of qualified participants to avoid recruitment shortfalls (the business case); improvement of military effectiveness in humanitarian missions and facilitation of civil-military cooperation; and integration of previously conflicted groups after a political turn-around. These may be understood, singly or in combination, to represent functional requirements or to otherwise reflect pressures for change to a more inclusive military, depending on the national context.

Added to these reasons are a number of others that accrue from the expanded talent pool of a diverse military workforce, including more innovation and creativity, an enhanced organizational image that will be attractive to the underutilized segments of the population, and improved satisfaction, morale, performance, and productivity in specific types of military operations. It may well be essential to the long-term health of the all-volunteer military in culturally and socially diverse democracies that a determined and comprehensive approach to diversity management be adopted.

GENDER INCLUSIVENESS AND THE FOURTH OPTION

Finally, it is important to provide several comments on gender diversity – or, more appropriately, gender inclusiveness – which has been our principal concern. Following others, authors of this volume have referred to the pervasiveness of the "combat masculine warrior model", "warrior frameworks", and "warrior creep" that have limited women's roles and employment and military careers. Analytic frameworks can help us understand the position in which women find themselves vis-à-vis male-dominated organizational regimes.

Feminist social theorists have examined the frameworks constructed by men to provide explanations of social phenomena presumed to apply to all of society, and they have found them wanting.[35] Interestingly, much of social theory has been focused on using "objective methods" to examine conditions and relationships that underlie social solidarity or cohesion and social conflict, without taking into account the inherent gender contradictions and conflicts. Many of the concepts used to assess gender diversity are rooted in traditional male perceptions of the world. This is particularly the case for explanations of change within the military. A recent organizational analysis, focused on women's participation in civilian enterprises applies equally to the military.[36] In the expansion of women's roles within the military and elsewhere, the underlying assumptions regarding "equitable" social arrangements have led to three identifiable approaches that will be familiar to many readers. These aim to (1) "fix the women" (i.e., re-socialize women to make them more like men in their traits and modus operandi); (2) "value the feminine" (i.e., celebrate the differences between men and women and allocate them to their stereotypical organizational roles); or (3) "create equal opportunities" (remove structural barriers to women's recruitment and advancement, through affirmative action, specified targets, and the like). The first two are based on assumptions of socialized gender differences that either have to be eliminated or used for role allocation in employment settings; the third is based on the perception of differential structures of opportunity and power blockages that are thought to be redressable through surface adjustments, without changing the fundamental cultural and social bases of traditional social relations. All of these carry with them disadvantages to women, since none is gender-neutral, even though some appear to be.[37] For a variety of reasons, although attempts to create equal opportunity have distinct benefits for women, none can remove the male power advantage in organizations, the military included.

The fourth option, suggested by Ely and Meyerson,[38] is a non-traditional approach that focuses on those areas where male dominance and male advantage need to be disrupted if progress toward *real equality* is to be made. It involves identifying and changing the "system of oppressive relations reproduced in and by social practices". Since these "relations" and "social practices" are based on assumptions that are taken-for-granted, their problematic nature is not self-evident and therefore they require close examination. Ely and Meyerson argue that this perspective should be applied to the examination of formal policies and procedures; informal work practices; norms and patterns of work; narratives, rhetoric, language, and other symbolic expressions; and informal patterns of everyday interaction.[39] These are highly relevant to women's participation in the military in general and in combat roles in particular. Among the important issues to be addressed is the social discourse surrounding women's alleged negative impact on social cohesion (and therefore operational effectiveness) that reinforces and helps to justify policy restrictions on their participation *both individually and as a group*.[40] Where masculinity is socially and culturally defined as essential to combat effectiveness and femininity is defined as existing in opposition, little progress in furthering gender inclusiveness is possible. Military analysts have only just begun to examine the models and assumptions underlying the traditional combat culture, and it is not coincidental that the leaders here are women.[41] Such an approach moves us away from traditional assumptions about operational imperatives and the like that act as blinders to socially constructed reality – including the construction of gender identities. In so doing, it is more likely to uncover the areas that place *most* women and *some* men at a disadvantage and thereby provide a basis for developing a genuine culture of gender-inclusiveness within the military.

As the military "transitions" toward more inclusiveness, new tools are being introduced elsewhere that promise to assist in implementing diversity models. One of these tools, labelled "gender-based" (or "diversity-based") analysis (GBA), and described by Davis,[42] is a more practitioner-oriented method of implementing gender- or diversity-inclusiveness. It is currently being used within various departments of government. Intended to include all women and men, GBA encompasses the broader issues of diversity management as well. Again, it is a method and a process that the military may well wish to utilize, in order to realize strategic inclusiveness goals on the policy, program, and practice levels.

CONCLUSION

It is clear that an inclusive model of military participation, which requires an effective diversity-management approach, is a long-term necessity for the military institutions of virtually all liberal democracies. While each has tackled the diversity issue in its own way, those in the forefront have a supportive legislative framework and a supportive strategic leadership approach that has seriously attempted to find the ways and provide the means to make diversity work. These appear to be minimal requirements for continuous long-term progress toward successful diversity management. There is a need to move beyond those concepts and ideas that continuously emphasize traditional, exclusive military models and toward inclusive models that better match the conditions that exist in post-modern society and the demands on military operational personnel. The overarching message in this volume is that transformational concepts and macro- and micro-policy, at least in the all-volunteer forces of Western democracies, should reflect social realities that exist both within and outside the military. Once again, also, it is suggested that to achieve further progress in gender diversity entails serious examination and modification of the hyper-masculine cultural environment of the operational segments of the military – most specifically the combat arms/infantry.

That militaries have made progress in diversity management over the past decade there can be no doubt. Two indicators are the greater acceptance of diversity among military members and the reduction in virtually all types of harassment (a form of discrimination) in the four Anglo-American nations compared in this volume. We may question, however, whether or not the way in which gender diversity is viewed fundamentally is equal to the task of determining the policy and practice arrangements that should exist to render the environment gender-inclusive in any meaningful sense. One of the problems is that women (as well as ethno-cultural groups) are not well represented in the more senior (that is, powerful) echelons of the military: largely a function of the internal selection and development systems that have a substantially masculine, mainstream social and cultural weighting. (This, in turn, is reflected in both recruitment and retention rates among non-mainstream groups.) As Ely and Meyerson suggest, a more fundamental, comprehensive, "disruptive" approach is necessary if men and women – or more broadly, the full range of gender types[43] – are ultimately to be placed on the same footing. Moskos is correct that gender and other types of diversity are qualitatively different issues and, to some extent, require different approaches. However, they are alike in two respects: first, both are ascriptive labels, around which have formed socially constructed identity characteristics that have placed them at a distinct disadvantage vis-à-vis the dominant military group(s); and, second, both require social and cultural transformation on the part of the military, which should be reflected in internal philosophies, policies, programs and practices. A successful, comprehensive diversity management approach for the military begins with, and is driven by, a *clearly articulated vision of inclusiveness and accommodation* of social and cultural differences, along with the necessary leadership and management supports – including appropriate evaluative tools – to ensure its effective implementation.

NOTES

1   Morris Janowitz, *The Professional Soldier* (Beverly Hills, CA: Sage, 1960, 1971).

2   See Charles C. Moskos, John A. Williams, and David R. Segal, eds., *The Post-Modern Military: Armed Forces After the Cold War* (New York: Oxford University Press, 2000); and Joseph Söeters, and Jan van der Meulen, eds., *Managing Diversity in the Armed Forces* (Amsterdam: Tilburg University Press, 1999): 212-214.

3   Charles Moskos and John Butler, *All That We Can Be* (New York: Basic Books, 1996).

4   For earlier examples of this tendency, see Franklin Pinch, "Military Manpower and Social Change: Assessing the Institutional Fit", *Armed Forces & Society* 8, 4 (Summer 1982): 575-600; Charles Cotton and Franklin Pinch, "The Winds of Change: Manning the Canadian Enlisted Force" in *Life in the Rank and File*, eds. David R. Segal and H. Wallace Sinaiko (Washington: Pergamon-Brassey's, 1986), 212-231.

5   David R. Segal and Meyer Kestnbaum, "Professional Closure in the Military Labor Market: A Critique of Pure Cohesion," in *The Future of the Army Profession*, ed. Lloyd J. Matthews (Washington: McGraw-Hill, 2002).

6   For Canadian examples, see Franklin C. Pinch, *Perspectives on Organizational Change in the Canadian Forces* (Arlington, VA: United States Research Institute for Behavioural and Social Sciences, 1994); Franklin C. Pinch, "Canada: Managing Change with Shrinking Resources", in *The Post-Modern Militar*, Moskos, Williams, and Segal, Chapter 9.

7   Samuel Huntington, *The Soldier and the State* (NewYork: Random House, 1957).

8   See Charles A. Cotton, Rodney Crook, and Franklin C. Pinch, "Canada's Professional Military: The Limits of Civilianization", *Armed Forces &Society*, Vol. 4, No. 3 (Spring/May 1978): 365-390; elaborated in Franklin Pinch, "Military Manpower and Social Change: Assessing the Institutional Fit", *Armed Forces & Society*, Vol. 8, No. 4 (Summer 1982): 575-600.

9   For a succinct summary, see David R. Segal and Mady W. Segal, "Change in the Military Organization", *Annual Review of Sociology*, 9: 151-170.

10   Morris Janowitz, "The Future of the Military Profession," in *War Morality and the Military Profession*, ed. Maltham M. Wakin.(Boulder: Westview Press, 197), 51-78.

11   See Peter Kasurak, "Civilianization and the Military Ethos: Civil-Military Relations in Canada," *Canadian Public Administration*, Vol. 25, No. 1 (Spring, 1982): 108-129; and Harriet Critchley, "Civilianization and the Military," *Armed Forces & Society*, Vol. 6, NO. 1 (Fall 1989): 117-136.

12   See Morris Janowitz, T*he Professional Soldier*, Second Edition (Prologue) Beverly Hills, CA:Sage, 1971), x-xii.

13   See Jason Dunn, *Women in the Combat Arms: A Question of Attitudes? Master's Thesis* (Ottawa: University of Ottawa, 1999); also Donna Winslow and Jason Dunn, "Women in the Canadian Forces: Between Legal and Social Integration," *Current Sociology*, Vol. 50, No.5 (2001): 641-647.

14   Henning Sorensen, "New Perspectives on the Military Profession: The I/O Model and Esprit de Corps Reevaluated," *Armed Forces & Societ*, Vol. 20, No. 4 (Summer 1994): 599-617.

15   For a critical analysis of both Janowitz and Huntington, see Peter D. Feaver, "The Civil-Military Problematique: Huntington, Janowitz, and the Question of Civilian Control," in *Armed Forces and Society*, Vol. 23, No. 2 (Winter)1996): 149-178.

15   Cited in Pinch, "Military Manpower": 585.

17   See Morris Janowitz and Charles Moskos, "Racial composition in the All-Volunteer Force", *Armed Forces & Society* (Fall 1974): 109-123.

18   Charles Moskos, "Institutional and Occupational Trends in Armed Forces," in *The Military: More than Just a Job?*, eds., C.C. Moskos and F.R. Wood (Washington: Pergamon-Brassey's, 1988), 15-26.

19   Charles Moskos, "Diversity in the Armed Forces of the United States," in *Managing Diversity in the Armed Force*, eds., Söeters and van der Meulen, 13-32.

20   See Franklin Pinch and David Segal, Postmodernism, Post-Modernity and Military Organization. (Kingston, ON: CF Leadership Institute, 2003).

21   Robin Ely and Debra Meyerson, "Theories of Gender in Organizations: A New Approach to Organizational Analysis and Change," Research in *Organizational Behaviour*, 22: 103-151.

22   Moskos, "Diversity in the Armed Forces," 29-30.

23   See, for example, R.A. Syde, *Natural Women Cultured Men: A Feminist Perspective on Sociological Theory* (Agincourt,ON: Methuen Publications, 1987); and Rachel Woodward and Patricia Winter, "Discourses of Gender in the British Army," *Armed Forces & Society*, Vol. 30, No. 2 (2004): 279-301.

24   See Karen Dunivin, "Military Culture: Change and Continuity," *Armed Forces & Society* (Summer, 1994): 531-548; Franklin Pinch, *Selected Issues and Constraints on Full Gender Integration in Elite Ground Combat Units in Canada* (Kingston: FCP Human Resources Consulting, 2002).

25   James Burk, "Theories of Democratic Civil-Military Relations," *Armed Forces & Society*, Vol. 29, No. 1(Fall 2002): 7-29.

26   Charles A. Cotton, "The Institutional Organization Model and the Military," in *The Military*, eds. Moskos and Wood, 39-58.

27   Major professional issues are summarized and discussed in Alan Okros, *Duty with Honour/ The Profession of Arms in Canada: Defining the Nature of the Military as a Profession* (Kingston, ON: CF Leadership Institute, 2003); leadership issues are summarized in Robert Walker, "Leadership Competencies Framework for the Canadian Forces," Draft Report (Kingston, ON: CF Leadership Institute, 2004).

28   Franklin Pinch, Lorne W. Bentley, and Phyllis P. Browne, *Research Program on the Military Profession: Background Considerations* (Kingston, ON: CF Leadership Institute, 2004).

29   This position is found in Pinch, *Selected Issues and Constraints*.

30   A significant part of the discussion on leadership is based on a series of papers that draw upon a wide range of leadership theory and empirical research sources, written by Karol Wenek as background for the development of the *Canadian Forces Leadership Manual*; Karol Wenek, *Institutional Challenge and Change in the 21st Century: The Road Ahead for Canadian Forces Leadership*, Paper delivered at the IUS Canada Conference, Kingston, Ontario, October 25-27, 2002; Defining Leadership (Kingston, ON: Canadian Forces Leadership Institute, 2002); *Defining Effective Leadership in the Canadian Forces: Content and Process Frameworks* (Kingston: Canadian Forces Leadership Institute, 2002); also, Karol Wenek and Robert Walker, *Leadership in the Canadian Forces: Doctrinal Principles, Draft Report* (Kingston: CF Leadership Institute, 2004).

31   Personal communication with Professor Donna Winslow. Also, see Donna Winslow, "Misplaced Loyalties: The Role of Military Culture in the Breakdown of Discipline in Peace Operations," *Canadian Review of Sociology and Anthropology*, Vol. 35, No. 3 (1998): 345-367.

32   Louise Gagnon and Jason Dunn, *Canadian Forces Diversity Climate Project: Analysis of 1999 Survey Qualitative Comment*s, TR 01-01 (Ottawa: National Defence Directorate of Human Resources Research and Evaluation, April 2001).

33   Nan Weiner, *Making Diversity Work* (Scarborough, ON: Carswell, 1997).

34   Söeters and van der Meulen, *Managing Diversity*, 212-214.

35   See, for example, Syde, *Natural Women Cultured Men*.

36   Ely and Meyerson, "Theories of Gender in Organizations".

37   See, for example, Mady W. Segal, "Women's Military Roles Cross-Nationally: Past, Present and Future" *Gender and Society*, Vol. 9, No. 6 (1995): 757-775; Woodward and Winter, "Discourses of Gender in the British Army".

38   Ely and Meyerson, "Theories of Gender in Organizations": 113.

39   Ibid.: 114 *et passim*.

40   Woodward and Winter, "Discourses of Gender in the British Army".

41   For example, see Dunivin, "Military Culture"; and Donna Winslow, *Canadian Warriors in Peacekeeping: Points of Tension in Complex Cultural Encounters* (Kingston, ON: CF Leadership Institute, 2003).

42   For a full discussion of the applications of gender-based analysis or GBA, see Karen Davis, *Gender-Based Analysis: A Potential Strategic Human Resource Tool*, D Strat HR Research Note 11/02 (Ottawa,: National Defence Headquarters Directorate of Strategic Human Resources, 2002).

43   This would include transgendered, gay, and lesbian persons who are typically stereotyped, discriminated against, excluded, or marginalized, including by the military. With the exception of a few of the more conservative Western democratic regimes, there are no formal restrictions on gays and lesbians; they may still be discriminated against and/or marginalized, however.

ABOUT THE CONTRIBUTORS

PHYLLIS BROWNE

Dr. Phyllis Browne is a graduate of McGill and Concordia universities in Montreal. She holds a doctoral degree in Sociology specializing in education, gender issues and labour markets. She is currently employed as a Defence Scientist by the Department of National Defence and is assigned to the Canadian Forces Leadership Institute of the Canadian Defence Academy in Kingston, Ontario.

KAREN DAVIS

Karen Davis is currently employed as a Senior Defence Scientist at the Canadian Forces Leadership Institute, following assignments as a strategic human resources analyst, diversity policy officer and applied research officer. She has conducted research in the Canadian Forces over the past 12 years on a range of human resource issues, predominantly in the areas of gender and diversity. Her research on women has focused on issues impacting attrition, integration of women into the combat arms, and gender-based analysis. The mother of 9-year-old Kelsy, Karen is also a member, and past executive member, of the Defence Women's Advisory Organization, and a retired Canadian Forces officer.

GWYN HARRIES-JENKINS

Professor Gwyn Harries-Jenkins was a United Kingdom State Scholar (1949-1953) who read law at the University of Wales and administrative law (droit administratif) at the College d'Europe, Bruges. Subsequently, he obtained his MA in European Law and History at the University of East Anglia (1967); MPhil in Sociology at UEA in (1968) and PhD at University of Hull (1977). He was commissioned as a regular officer in the Royal Air Force in 1953, serving in Europe and the Far East. (General Service Medal: Malay Peninsula) On transfer to the retired list in 1970, he joined the University of Hull where he was successively Director of Adult Education and Dean of the School of Continuing Education. Currently, he is Director of the Hull based Comparative Research on Military Institutions Project (CRMI) which he co-founded with Professor Morris Janowitz in 1972. The most recent CRMI Project, funded by the US Army Research Institute, was the analysis of the extended role of women in armed forces (March 2002).

NICOLA HOLDEN

Nicola Holden holds an Honours Bachelor of Arts degree in Psychology and Sociology from Wilfrid Laurier University and a Masters of Arts degree from the University of Waterloo. Her main focus was family and gender. She has been employed with the Department of National Defence since 1999 as a Defence Scientist. She has carried out research on gender integration and harassment in the Canadian Forces and in international militaries. Her main area of expertise is sociological and statistical research and analysis of employment equity issues for the Canadian Forces.

CHRISTIAN LEUPRECHT

Christian Leuprecht is Assistant Professor in the Department of Political Science and Economics and the Division of Distance and Continuing Studies at the Royal Military College of Canada and cross-appointed to the Department of Political Studies at Queen's University. He is also a research associate at the Institute of Intergovernmental Relations in the School of Policy Studies at Queen's University and a research fellow of the Queen's Centre for International Relations. His expertise is the area of comparative political demography.

ALLISTER MACINTYRE

Lieutenant Colonel Allister MacIntyre has been with the Canadian Forces Leadership Institute since 2001, where he presently serves as the Deputy Director. He holds a doctoral degree in Social Psychology and a Master's degree in Organizational Psychology from Queen's University. He has worked as a researcher in Canada and Australia and taught psychology for three years at Royal Roads

Military College. His academic and research interests include leadership, climate and culture, cohesion, and work stress. He is the current Chair of the Psychology in the Military section of the Canadian Psychological Association, and presently holds positions as an adjunct professor of psychology at Carleton University and the University of Guelph.

KATHLEEN MACLAURIN

Kathleen MacLaurin, who holds a dual graduate degree in criminology and sociology, has been a policy analyst with the Canadian Department of National Defence and Justice Canada, where she has been involved in examining Aboriginal issues, including those related to implementation of the Youth Criminal Justice Act and the Employment Equity Plan (Department of National Defence). She is currently a policy advisor on counter-terrorism with the International Crime and Terrorism Division of Foreign Affairs Canada, with responsibilities for the development of Asia-Pacific counter-terrorism policy, the establishment of counter-terrorism capacity-building programming and international military/police counter-terrorism relations. She has an abiding interest in Aboriginal diversity issues, especially those relate to institutional accommodation of value differences.

BRIAN MCKEE

Brian Mc Kee is a Senior Defence Scientist with the Department of National Defence, Canada. He has undergraduate degrees in Sociology and Anthropology from Queens University, Belfast and a graduate degree in Sociology from Carleton University, Ottawa.

ALAN OKROS

Dr. Alan Okros is presently an Associate Professor with the Military Psychology and Leadership Department of the Royal Military College. He holds a doctoral degree in Industrial/Organizational Psychology from the University of Waterloo. A former member of the Canadian Forces, his CF positions have included Commanding Officer, Canadian Forces Personnel Applied Research Unit, Director Personnel Research Team (now Human Resource Research and Evaluation), Director of Strategic Human Resource Analysis, and the Director of the Canadian Forces Leadership Institute. He is the author of numerous publications on Human Resource issues.

FRANKLIN PINCH

Dr. Franklin Pinch, a sociologist and human resources professional, is an internationally recognized scholar and analyst of the impact of social change on organization, human resource management and leadership and professionalism within the military institution. Over the past three decades, he has authored, co-authored or edited reports, articles, book chapters and books, and has also provided a range of research-based consultation services, in virtually all of these topic areas. His most recent works deal with post-modern trends, change issues in military professionalism and senior leader perceptions, trends in military sociology in Canada, and barriers to full gender integration within the military. Currently a Research Associate at the Queen's University School of Policy Studies and a private consultant, Dr. Pinch was formerly a Senior Research Fellow at the Canadian Forces Leadership Institute.

KATIA SORIN

Dr. Katia Sorin holds a doctorate degree in sociology from Paris I Panthéon-Sorbonne University. She has undertaken research on gender integration both in France and Canada, and on leadership roles. In 2003, she published a book at L'Harmattan (Paris) : *Femmes en armes : une place introuvable ? Le cas de la féminisation des armées françaises*. She is associated with the Georges Friedmann Laboratory.